D0617389

# THE AMERICAN MASTERS FLY FISHING SYMPOSIUM

## *Part Two - Tackle*

*Featuring:*

Dan Blanton
Gary Borger
Lefty Kreh
Flip Pallot
John Randolph
Jim Teeny
Dave Whitlock

ODYSSEUS EDITIONS
*Birmingham, Alabama*

THE AMERICAN MASTERS FLY FISHING SYMPOSIUM
PART TWO — TACKLE

Published by Odysseus Editions, Inc. under the direction of:

Leslie B. Adams, President & Publisher

Bernard "Lefty" Kreh, Editor-in-Chief

Amanda P. Adams, Vice President

Linda Grantham, Administration

John Randolph, Editorial Consultant

Robin McDonald, Designer

Rod Walinchus, Illustrator

Harry Middleton, Contributing Editor

FRONTISPIECE: *Participants at the American Masters Fly Fishing Symposium.* From left to right, top row: *Dan Blanton, Leslie Adams (Publisher), Dave Whitlock;* middle row: *John Randolph, Flip Pallot, Gary Borger;* front row, *Lefty Kreh, Jim Teeny.*

# CONTENTS

OVERLEAF: *Tarpon fly patterns.*

# INTRODUCTION

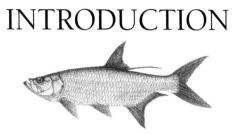

The first American Masters Fly Fishing Symposium took place in Denver, Colorado, on August 21 and 22, 1991. In addition to myself, the fly-fishing professionals that participated were Dan Blanton, one of California's premier fly fishermen, particularly in big game saltwater fishing; Gary Borger, one of the top trout fishermen and stream entomologists in the world, with regional midwestern expertise from his home waters of Minnesota; Flip Pallot, a top Florida Keys guide and one of the principal instructors at the Florida Keys Fly Fishing School; John Randolph, Editor and Publisher of our leading fly-fishing magazine, *Fly Fisherman*, and an expert in all aspects of American trout fishing; Oregon's Jim Teeny, generally acknowledged to be the country's leading steelhead and Pacific salmon fisherman; and Dave Whitlock, Arkansas' celebrated bass, trout and stream entomology expert.

The agenda for the two-day Symposium was based upon a series of questions about all aspects of fresh and saltwater fly fishing that had been submitted to us in advance by a large group of amateur American fly fishermen in response to a mail questionnaire that had been sent out by the Publisher of the Library, Les Adams. Prior to our meetings, Les and I evaluated the questionnaires we had received with a view to selecting those questions that appeared to be the most frequently asked or the most important, or both; and we organized them into three major subject categories: skills, tackle, and travel and the fly-fishing life.

The Symposium now continues with the book which you have before you, as the professionals examine the second major subject category, fly-fishing tackle — reels, rods, lines, knots, and flies.

The tackle aspect of fly fishing is really interesting to me. I confess to being a tackle freak, and I think most fly fishermen are. I'm not sure why that is. Fly-fishing tackle includes a lot of gadgets, and I know that most men are gadget-oriented. And I know, also, that despite all the efforts that are being made to bring more women into the sport — an effort, incidentally, that I enthusiastically support — fly fishing is still predominantly a male activity. I'm not sure why that is, either.

A good friend of mine, who's an expert at marketing, made what I think was a real insightful observation about this. He thinks unlike women, whom he believes like to acquire one whole thing at one time, *men like to acquire things in parts over a long period of time*. He may be right, since a lot of the leisure activities that men seem to prefer — maintaining an automobile, owning and equipping a boat, acquiring stereo equipment, building and refinishing furniture, and of course, fly fishing — involve acquiring and working with a lot of small parts.

All my life I have been fooling around with every piece of fly-fishing tackle — or every fly-fishing gadget — that I could lay my hands on, hoping, I suppose, that I could learn how it worked, or seeing if I could think of a way of improving it, or trying to invent a new or alternative design for it that would make fly fishing more productive and enjoyable for me and my readers.

Those of you who know me, or have read anything I've written, know that I'm a big advocate for what I like to call "modern fly fishing." By that I mean, of course, retaining all the grand traditions of sportsmanship that are associated with fly fishing, but at the same time, using to our advantage the great twentieth-century fly-fishing tackle technology that is available to us now. Such words as monofilament, graphite, strike indicator, Crystal Flash, shooting taper, and so on, didn't even exist — at least in a fly-fishing context — in the old days. And while some people may argue that fly fishing was more enjoyable then — in the sense that it was simpler and less technology-driven — nobody can say it was better, if better means catching more and bigger fish, which is what I think it means for most of us!

Because today, *without sacrificing any of the worthwhile fly-fishing traditions*, I believe the average fly fisherman is casting better, fishing better, and enjoying a higher fish-per-day success rate than his ancestors. And the development and proper use of modern tackle is one of the principal reasons.

So if you're into this tackle aspect of fly fishing anywhere nearly as much as I am, I think you're going to enjoy this little book very much, as it's crammed with a lot of great ideas from these top professionals about what tackle they equip themselves with and how they use it. Good reading. And good fly fishing!

OVERLEAF: *Readying rods for a day of winter fly fishing.*

# CHAPTER ONE

# RODS

*What rods do you recommend for fresh and saltwater
fly fishing, and what should be their line weight, length,
and construction?*

DAVE WHITLOCK — Are you asking what rods we would
choose for our personal use, or what we would recommend for someone else? I would recommend an 8 1/2-
foot rod in line size 7 for most average people, but I
wouldn't choose that for myself, you know, I would do
something a little different.

LEFTY KREH — Let's talk about your personal choices first.

DAVE WHITLOCK — Well, primarily, I'd use a 7-foot 2-
weight rod, an 8 or 8 1/2-foot 5-weight rod, and an 8
3/4-foot 8-weight rod.

LEFTY KREH — How would you use these three sizes?

DAVE WHITLOCK — The 2-weight rod would be for trout or
sunfish or anything on any type of water that small flies
are required on.

The 5-weight would be primarily for fishing for trout
and bass in intermediate waters with nymphs, larger dry
flies, small streamers, and small Woolly Buggers.

The 8-weight would cover all of my saltwater fishing
and all of my larger freshwater fishing. I like the 8 3/4-foot
length, because it fits my physical structure better.

JOHN RANDOLPH — I agree, except I would rather have my 8-weight rod at 9 feet.

GARY BORGER — Well, I'd choose a whole range of rods.

I'd have an 8-foot rod in line weights 3 and 4 for most of my light-line work, basically using a 3-weight line most of the time. Because by double hauling, I can fish anything with that rod all the way up to about a #2 Strip Leech. So I can cover a lot of sins with that thing.

I'd have an 8-foot rod for line size 5 or 6, probably in one of the new three or four-piece travel designs. Because again, with a 5 or 6-weight, you can cover a whole lot of things. It's sort of a nice, all-around size for traveling.

I'd also have an another rod in size 5 or 6, but at 8 1/2 feet. That's sort of my big gun rod for trout — for normal trout, not for steelhead. Because with that rod I can really whang out some big flies.

I'd have a 9-foot rod for line size 7 or 8 that I would use on big steelhead, small salmon, for bass fishing — that sort of thing.

I would have a 9 or 9 1/2-foot rod in a line size of 9 or 10. That would be for bass popping, bigger salmon — Kings and such — as well as saltwater work.

And finally, if I were going after tarpon or something, I'd go for a 9-foot rod in a line size of 11 or 12, probably with about a 13 to 14-weight butt on it, a little stiffer and heavier butt.

DAN BLANTON — I don't fish for trout as much as these other guys, but I do like trout fishing. I would have a 4-weight rod for the light end. I don't go lighter than that because I can't see the flies that you guys use with the lighter-weight lines.

Then I would fish a 6-weight rod for pretty much all the other kinds of trout fishing I do, because, as Gary said, you can throw just about any type of fly up to a very large Woolly Bugger with a 6-weight.

For larger lakes — like big lakes where you need to throw longer or encounter windy conditions — I would use an 8 or 9-weight rod, and the 9-weight would transcend into my steelhead fishing and a lot of my King salmon fishing. A lot of guys would fish a lighter rod for these fish — maybe an 8-weight — but I think the 9-weight is probably a better choice, again, because of the wind and for the occasional need to use heavily weighted flies. Also, the 9-weight would handle almost all my light saltwater fishing — bonefishing, small tarpon, and such.

For the bigger end of saltwater, I would have an 11-weight for tarpon for those real calm days when you have to throw a lighter line. Because sometimes you can spook a tarpon with a big line.

And then for the really big stuff, under normal conditions, with normal winds, I would use a 12 or 13-weight rod for big tarpon and billfish. Today most of the top quality 12 or 13-weight rods have enough butt to handle anything that I would want to latch onto with a fly rod.

JIM TEENY — I'm sold on graphite.

LEFTY KREH — Yes. Is there anybody here that doesn't like graphite? Yes, we all like graphite.

JIM TEENY — My light-rod choice would be, for bass and bluegills and smaller trout, an 8-foot 4-weight rod.

A 9-foot 6-weight rod is one of my favorite intermediate rods. I would use that for a lot of trout fishing.

Then when I get into the steelhead, I love the 9 1/2-foot 8-weight rod. It's a real good, all-around rod.

And when I get into my King salmon and big steelhead fishing, or if I were going to really big water, like that of the Skeena river system in British Columbia, for example, my choice would be a 10-foot 9-weight rod.

For tarpon, I would use a 9-foot 12-weight rod.

FLIP PALLOT — For freshwater, I would probably just borrow stuff from John!

For saltwater, I think I would have a 6-weight rod for a lot of bonefishing — particularly in the deep tropics.

I would have an 8-weight rod for larger bonefish, permit, snook, small tarpon — that sort of thing.

At the large end, I wouldn't use anything heavier than an 11-weight rod for tarpon, sailfish, and species like that. I have lately begun to believe that the larger rods are really much more than what's needed; and certainly, much more than what the average angler can handle. I mean, casting a 12-weight rod is beyond the ability of 99 percent of the people that I ever guide.

The 11-weight rod is a pretty deadly thing if you learn how to use it right, and it's a lot more fun to carry around than a 12 or 13-weight!

And in no instance would I consider these new 20-weight rods the manufacturers are beginning to fool with. I don't even think that's fly fishing anymore.

DAVE WHITLOCK — Good for you! I agree with that!

LEFTY KREH — You're referring to the new 20-pound IGFA class they're working with now?

JOHN RANDOLPH — What do they mean by that?

LEFTY KREH — It means that the tippet can't be stronger than 20-pound test. But Johnny, when Flip and I are photographing jumping tarpon, I'll have Flip just hook the fish with a 20-pound tippet joined to a heavy shock leader, which allows him to hold the fish tightly so that it really can't go anywhere and as a result, it will just blast out of the water over and over again! That's okay for specialized photography purposes, but it's a totally unethical use for real fly fishing, as far as I am concerned.

JOHN RANDOLPH — I agree with that!

LEFTY KREH — My favorite trout rod is a 3-weight rod, and I use it in any delicate or light-line conditions. For me, a 2-weight rod is just a little bit on the light side. Now some people tell me they can't cast flies well with such light fly lines. But you should keep in mind that in a 3-weight line, the first 30 feet weighs 100 grains. And with that much weight, you can throw anything, except heavy Woolly Buggers or nymphs, for quite a long way.

If I could only have two trout rods, I would have a 3-weight and a 6-weight. I find that with these two weights, I can throw pretty well most any kind of fly I want.

I like an 8-weight rod, too, for lots of things. In fact, if I had to have just one rod, I would simply take an 8-weight and use lighter lines as the fishing conditions require. That's something else that we might want to talk about later. About how many lines you can use on the same rod, because it's something a lot of people don't realize.

DAVE WHITLOCK — That's a good point!

LEFTY KREH — And going back to Flip's point about heavy rods, I recall writing in the second edition of my saltwater book that I thought there would be a drastic change over the next few years back toward 10 and 11-weight rods for tarpon fishing, with the possible exception of tarpon fishing at Homosassa, where you are going to encounter 150-pound fish.

I think the new rods that some of the manufacturers are coming out with — Sage is one with which I am most familiar since I work with them a lot — have heavier butts than before. So that a 10 or 11-weight rod can now be just as strong as many of the older 12-weight rods. And of course, they are so much easier to cast. And since the lines are lighter, you'll spook fish on the cast less often. Most tarpon anglers are making a mistake, I think, in continuing to use the big 12 and 13-weight rods.

DAN BLANTON — Also, a lot of people I've watched think it's great sport and a sign of considerable skill to fish ultra-light tackle. They under-tackle their fish. Now if you know how to fight a fish with a 10 or an 11-weight rod, you can beat big fish in a sportsmanlike way most of the time so that the fish can be released in healthy condition. But sometimes I see saltwater anglers taking what seems forever — an hour or even two hours — to land a fish that should have been landed in 30 minutes! I've seen people who are actually proud of themselves for landing a 100-pound tarpon on a 9-weight rod! Well, I doubt seriously that tarpon lived after it was released. It was shark bait!

So one of the reasons that I still use the 12 and 13-weight Big Berthas, especially in windy conditions, is that I can beat a fish fast with that size rod.

*Do you like short rods — 7 feet long or less? What are their advantages and disadvantages versus longer rods?*

DAVE WHITLOCK — Well, I don't normally use rods shorter than 7 feet. In fact, 7 1/2 feet is about it. Shorter rods are sort of fun to use, but they definitely handicap your casting, except in tight places where the length of the rod interferes with the casting stroke. Rods up to about 9 feet long, I think, are extremely efficient. But once you get past 9 feet, I think length becomes a handicap, because even a 3-weight rod gets pretty heavy at a length of 9 1/2 or 10 feet. I know that for myself, the longer the rod gets, the more mistakes I make. It's easier to screw up on timing. So I prefer to stay within the 8 to 9-foot range of rod for my fishing.

JOHN RANDOLPH — I feel the same way, with the exception of fly fishing in many of our eastern streams. In the heavy brush that grows there, a 7-foot rod is almost a must.

DAVE WHITLOCK — That's an example of a place where the rod just can't be moved.

LEFTY KREH — I call that tunnel fishing. But you know — and I've mentioned this tip several times in my previous books — if you have an 8-foot rod and you are in a tight place, you can put your hand up by the butt stripping guide and make the cast and create the casting effect of a shorter rod.

GARY BORGER — I like rods 7 1/2 to 9 1/2 feet long, period!

LEFTY KREH — I like rods 7 1/2 to 9 feet long, too. And aside from casting considerations, I also feel that using rods less than 7 feet long is, in a way, not as sportsmanlike for fly fishing. We all know that when hardware fishermen go offshore for giant tuna and billfish, they will never use a long rod to fight those big fish. Because, of course, it's much more efficient — if killing efficiently rather than sport is what you've after — to fight fish with short rods. Because the shorter the lever, the more pressure you can apply to the fish.

The way I like demonstrate that to people is to take a 12-inch ruler and hold it like a fly rod and press down on the far end. It will barely bend, no matter how much force

I apply. But then I take a yardstick, and when I press down on one end, I can begin to achieve a fair amount of bend. So when you use a short rod you are not more sporting, you are actually less sporting, if you are concerned about that type of ethic.

I think that short rods also complicate casting. I recall once writing a magazine piece listing 17 reasons why I thought longer fly rods fish better than shorter models.

DAN BLANTON — I agree with what Lefty just said. He's absolutely right. I favor my rods in a length of from 8 1/2 to 9 feet. I recognize that there are the occasional special circumstances where you need to have a shorter rod for telecasting, or a rod longer than that for mending and handling line or keeping your back cast above back brush, and things like that.

But one of the disadvantages of using a very long rod, I find when I'm fishing out of a boat, is that this long length makes it much more difficult to bring the fish to the net. Also, the longer rod is a disadvantage in fighting the larger gamefish. I think when you use a rod as long 10 or 10 1/2 feet, you have a hard time lifting big fish. You have to really pull the rod to achieve a 180-degree bend so you can handle them up close.

Additionally, with the very long rod, you have much more mass to move through the air, and when you are trying to stop that tip with the good casting technique that we have talked about, it is more difficult to do.

So I think the average 8 1/2 to 9-foot rod is probably the best length.

JIM TEENY — Do I have the floor?

LEFTY KREH — You have the floor and you can badmouth all of us!

JIM TEENY — I'm five feet six inches tall, and I prefer a 10-foot rod! I also like the 8 1/2 to 9 1/2-foot rods, but I favor the 10 for steelhead and salmon because I have to do a lot of roll casting. I really like the extra lift and height that I can get from it. I can put line out there a little easier, and it offers me a little bit more control. That extra half-foot or foot really does help me.

I used to use mostly 8-foot rods. But once I went steelhead fishing with Lani Waller, who had 9-1/2 footer. I was roll casting like a champion but he said, "Jim, Jesus Christ! You can't cast across this river with a 8-footer, here . . . try my rod!" And I said, "No, that's okay! I'm happy with my 8." And he said, "No, will you just try it?" And so I did. I picked up that 9 1/2-foot rod and roll casted that line. And I mean it was unbelievably easier than I had anticipated, much easier to cast with than my 8-footer! So, the next day I ordered a 9 1/2-foot rod.

DAVE WHITLOCK — That's why Atlantic salmon fishermen use 14-foot two-handed rods, for that same reason, the roll casting requirement.

DAN BLANTON — Do you use that long rod from a boat when you're salmon fishing? You know, like we do in California when we're fishing mostly from prams?

JIM TEENY — I don't do much pram fishing. My fishing is mostly river fishing, actual moving-current type of water.

LEFTY KREH — You're either at water level or in the water.

JIM TEENY — Yeah, I mean, I'm either wading or I'm right up close to shore.

DAN BLANTON — Yeah, because in a pram you can't lift a big King to the net with that big long rod.

JIM TEENY — Well, I can understand that the longer the rod, the harder it is to get those fish in. But where I've grown up, if you don't roll cast, there's about 60 or 70 percent of the water that you can't fish to! You just can't do it! So I've developed my roll cast so that it's probably my best and most accurate cast. I can put that fly anywhere with a roll cast.

LEFTY KREH — Well, I think roll casting, once you learn it, is the most accurate of all casts. Would most of you agree with that?

DAN BLANTON — It's the first cast that I teach. It's the easiest cast to learn and the first cast that you're going to do. You're going to roll cast to straighten your line, and if it's a sinking line, you're going to roll it to the surface with a roll cast.

LEFTY KREH — Flip, what do you think about rod size?

FLIP PALLOT — In saltwater, I think the best rod length is from 8 to a maximum of 9 feet. I don't know that I agree about shorter rods being tougher on fish. I think it's what you do with the rod. I think if you try to fight a big fish like you would a small trout — you know, where you hold the rod straight up over your head and only use the tip of the rod to fight fish — you're doing a great disservice to the fish with any length rod. But if you keep even a 9 or 10-foot rod low and use only the butt of the rod in fighting the fish, I think you shorten the lever.

DAVE WHITLOCK — Lefty, let me add just one or two more thoughts. Everybody recognizes that rod length is important to mending. It certainly is important, but the people

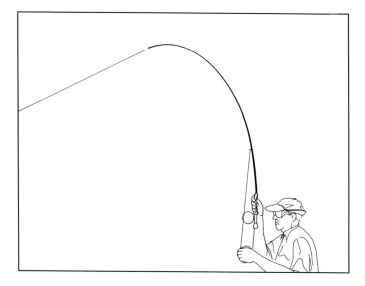

*Vertical Rod Position Only Applies Tip Pressure*

I have fished with who have mending problems don't have them because of rod length. Whether they were using a 7-foot or a 12-foot rod, they don't how to use the rod — regardless of its length — in making their mend. They simply flip the tip over rather than lifting up and coming over. A person of normal height with an 8-foot rod can mend 20 or 30 feet of line efficiently if he knows how to do it. But if you put a 10-foot rod in his hand, and if he just gives it a little flip, he still won't be mending properly.

Another thing about mending is that the stiffness of the rod is in direct proportion to how well you can mend with it. Russ Peak, one of the country's leading rod makers, was building some rods for me one time, and I had him build me a rod that was 10 1/2 feet long. I called it a manipula-tor. The first one he built for me was so soft, I couldn't mend as well with it as I could with one of my old 8

1/2-foot rods. But then he built me one that was real, real stiff. That was one of the first graphite rods he ever built, and I could mend incredibly well with that, you know!

LEFTY KREH — It didn't collapse on the tip. Well, let's move to that subject.

## What is rod action?

DAVE WHITLOCK — Well, I think all of us pretty well agree that how deeply a rod flexes is what we refer to as rod action. To me, a slow-action rod is one that once you have reached a full bend in the rod, it takes longer for the tip to recover back to that point where it was straight. With a faster-action rod, while the whole rod may bend, it recovers very quickly. Of course, some manufacturers vary the strength of the rod so that it bends differently throughout its length . . . so that it's not parabolic. So simply put, I think there is a slow rod, a medium-slow rod, a fast rod, and an extra-fast action rod. Those are more or less the rod actions that are popular now.

LEFTY KREH — Is there any one that you prefer?

DAVE WHITLOCK — That depends upon the fishing situation. For example, I think that all 2-weight rods should have an extra-slow action.

LEFTY KREH — The lighter the rod, the slower the action?

DAVE WHITLOCK — Primarily. With the smaller fly rod, the more delicate a fly presentation you have to make, or the more you want to put a fly softly on the water at close distance, the slower its action should be. But the farther you throw a fly, the bigger the fly, and the harder you have to set the hook, the faster or more powerful the action needs to be.

JOHN RANDOLPH — I agree with all that.

JIM TEENY — You covered that very well!

LEFTY KREH — Good! I think what Dave says is exactly right. When you want delicate presentations, and you're working close-in, the softer rods are the best choice. For example, some of the manufacturers are now making a slow trout rod and a real fast trout rod. Now, I fish with the slower rods all the time. But when you've got to transport the fly a long distance, or are facing difficult wind conditions, I think you can't get a rod that's too stiff. With a stiffer rod, if you accelerate your stroke, you can make a faster cast. But you can't take a real slow rod and make a fast accelerating stroke. So in tough casting conditions, the slower rods will hurt you, I think.

GARY BORGER — The way I define action is the way the rod flexes during the casting stroke. Then you also have to remember that a fishing rod isn't just a casting tool. It's also a fish-fighting tool. But when we talk about action, you know, basically we are talking about casting, not about fighting fish.

I define rod action in three ways: tip-action rods, medium-action rods, and full-flex rods. Tip-action means that during the casting stroke the upper one-quarter or so of the rod bends; in the medium-action rod the upper one-half to three-fifths bends; and with the full-flex rod, most all of the rod bends during the casting stroke.

Obviously, the tip-action rod moves faster because less of it is moving. Even if the graphite material is slow, it's still going to recover much more quickly than a rod that flexes all the way to the cork. And, I have to agree with

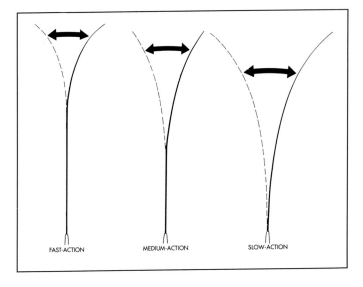

FAST-ACTION     MEDIUM-ACTION     SLOW-ACTION

*Rod Actions*

Dave, that when I am fishing light-line rods, I prefer to go to slightly slower actions, not necessarily for fly delivery but for playing the fish. It's really for both. But I want a rod that's more like Dick Swan's noodle rod, you know? You can land steelhead on a 2-pound line with that rod!

LEFTY KREH — But tell them what a noodle rod is . . .

GARY BORGER — Well, they are basically 12 to 14-foot rods designed to handle a 2-pound test line. With this type rod, if you stand normally and hold the rod out in a normal position, the tip will droop until it touches the floor, just like a giant piece of soft spaghetti! I mean, when you get a big fish on, and you hold that rod up, the tip actually bends right around and touches the butt when you're playing the fish! It's so much of a noodle that the fish never breaks you off. But it takes you two hours to land a fish, and I'm not really terribly excited about fishing with one of these rods. Like Dan, I think you are undergunned with these big fish — you're talking about 15-pound steelhead on 2-pound test line!

DAVE WHITLOCK — I call it nagging the fish.

GARY BORGER — So for the lighter lines, I tend to favor slightly more flex in the rod. And then you also have to consider how the actual bend of the rod occurs during the casting stroke. You can have a rod that's a little stiffer in the tip and softer in the middle, and still have a medium-action rod.

So there are a lot of things involved in action, and that raises the question of why rod manufacturers can't describe and standardize rod action? They could label the action of the rod — tip-action, medium-action, full-flex, and so on. But then, within that range, you could have a rod that was more parabolic, less parabolic — all sorts of other things.

LEFTY KREH — I think that's an impossible thing to do . . .

JIM TEENY — I really like rods that have a stiff butt section with its sensitivity mostly toward the tip. I have never been real fond of the rods in which I can feel the flex in the handle while I'm casting. You know what I mean?

LEFTY KREH — I hate those full-flex rods! I can't cast accurately with them. I feel like I have lost all control when they flop all over the place.

DAN BLANTON — We have heard some terms here — fast, medium, slow, parabolic — but one of the problems about this is that all of us here, as well as the rod manufacturers, use different terms to describe rod action. I think it's important that people understand that when they use the expression, "fast-tip," they are referring to the action of the tip in just flexing down a third or less of the rod length, and that medium-action, as we have already said, means flexing down midway. But some of the rod manufacturers refer to action as high-modulus, low-modulus, high-line speed, low-line speed, and so on, making it even more confusing to people.

I prefer rods that have anywhere from a medium to a faster action. In other words, the tip works more than the rest of the rod, or perhaps down to just half of its length. I really think that the caster can recover from mistakes much easier with what we call a high-modulus design, meaning that the rod returns from full flex to its original state very rapidly, regardless of how far it bends, because you can make a correction so much easier and gain greater versatility with this type rod.

But there are exceptions. If you take that high-speed rod with its incredibly fast return rate and fish a spring creek with a 7 or 8X-tippet, you won't be able to land any fish. I know I can't land any fish. I break everything off. So for spring creek fishing, I have to go to a slower rod in order to avoid doing that.

DAVE WHITLOCK — You break them off while you're setting the hook or while you're fighting them?

DAN BLANTON — While I'm setting the hook. Boom! . . . the fish is off!

LEFTY KREH — Would all of you agree that rods that are either very slow or very fast are the most difficult rods to cast and fish with?

DAVE WHITLOCK — Well, yes, because they require more precise technique.

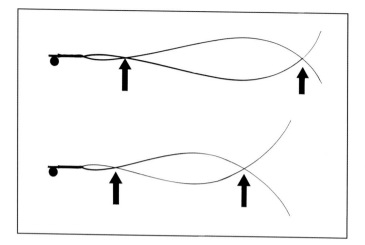

*Nodal Points on a Rod — The arrows indicate the nodal points of two rods. The closer the nodal point is to the tip the faster the rod. Thus, the upper rod has a much faster action than the lower rod.*

LEFTY KREH — I think, fortunately, that in the last ten years there are very few real slow rods being made. I think they were so bad that the rod manufacturers simply gave up on manufacturing them.

I think also that most of us would agree that for light-line fishing, you can fish so much better with a medium-action rod.

FLIP PALLOT — The only comment I have is that if we are going to use the technical terms, Lefty, we ought to get them right. The modulus is the amount of graphite mixed with the fiber glass. And the higher the modulus, the stiffer the rod is. But that doesn't have to do with where the nodal point occurs on the rod, which is the point at which the rod flexes — as Gary was talking about — the distance back from the tip, where the rod flexes.

I think what I am hearing is that everyone prefers the nodal point to be further toward the tip of the rod, which gives you a slightly faster action. The further toward the rod handle the nodal point is situated, the slower the action is, until you can actually get the nodal point back under the cork where you don't like to feel it.

So, sometimes it's fun to use real slow rods, but other times the faster rods are nicer. Generally, I think the fast rods are great fighting tools, but they are not so much fun to cast. You can certainly cast them, but a stiff 12 or a 13-weight rod is not a great casting rod.

LEFTY KREH — It's a fish-fighting tool. Dave, do you have something?

DAVE WHITLOCK — Well, when the 2-weight rods came out, there was an awful lot of bad press about the fact that extra-light rods were fish killers, which I believed at the time, because I thought I couldn't put enough pressure on a fish to fight and bring it in on a 2-weight.

But finally, after I had been using 2-weights for a little while, I changed my mind later while I was fishing the Bighorn River. On previous trips to the Bighorn, I had always used a 3, 4, or 5-weight rod, but I found this time that I was as able to land big fish faster with that 2-weight than I could on a 5-weight.

And what I have figured out — and I want your opinions on this because I think it is important to this discussion — is that you can put more pressure on the fish, more forgiving pressure, with a 2-weight rod, because the rod is so soft, and you won't tear the hook out of a fish's mouth as badly.

LEFTY KREH — Oh, I agree!

DAVE WHITLOCK — Do you all agree with that? If I tell somebody I can whip a big fish down on a 7X-tippet and a #20 fly with a 2-weight rod faster than I can with 5-weight, he will say, "No way, no way . . . you can't." But I can! I swear, I can!

GARY BORGER — Let me just point out one thing, Dave. The reason for that is because you're Dave Whitlock! The average person won't be able do it. If you give the average person a 2-weight rod, he will immediately assume a vertical rod position and stand there for an hour and not do anything. But you know how to fight fish. You know how to use the rod butt.

A 2-weight rod is better on the fish than a 5-weight, because the 2-weight does not allow you to create too much jolting pressure. So it's a better tool — for trout anyway — because you can put more flex in the rod and have a better shock-absorber effect when the fish shakes its head or something. So I agree with you.

DAVE WHITLOCK — The next question is, can that be extrapolated into fighting big fish on more flexible tackle?

DAN BLANTON — Dave, let me give you an example. I have fished for striped bass in San Francisco Bay since I was 15 years old — and that's a lot of years! When I first started fly fishing there, I only fished areas around piling structure. Over the course of almost 30 years, one of the best rods I ever used for that type fishing was the first saltwater rod manufactured by Fenwick, their model FF114. It was a very, very slow rod for the time. It flexed almost all the way into the butt. And the only way I could land 15 to 20-pound striped bass — anything over that weight I couldn't handle — was to literally hand-strip those fish out from the pilings. I found that with this slow rod, if I could keep a full bend in the rod, it would act like a big shock absorber and I could lean hard and strip and pull. I turned hundreds of 15 to 20-pound striped bass from the pilings with that rod.

FLIP PALLOT — I think nothing could be farther from the case for fighting big strong, fast, running fish. Bend is the last thing you want. All of you know how much stretch you can get in your backing and fly line and leader. With a big fish out at 50 or 75 yards, the last thing you need, in addition to the stretch in these components of your line, is even more stretch with a big bend in a rod. I think the more you can shorten the lever that you are fighting with — that is to say the more you can point the rod at the fish and use just the butt — the better off you are. When I'm fighting a big fish, the front two-thirds of the rod is perfectly straight, pointing at the fish. The whole bend is back in the fat, meaty, heavy-duty part of the rod. Otherwise you're liable to destroy the hoop strength of the rod and encourage breakage, particularly with graphites.

GARY BORGER — I might point out to you, Flip, that that's exactly the way we play big fish with a 2-weight rod.

FLIP PALLOT — No, Gary, I think we're talking about something else here. First of all, on trout you're fighting at fairly close proximity. You don't have the big stretch factors in your line.

GARY BORGER — That's what I'm saying, that we're using exactly the same technique that you use. We use the butt of the rod to fight the fish.

FLIP PALLOT — No, I'm addressing what Dave was talking about and what . . .

LEFTY KREH — Yeah, there's a difference, Gary! The difference is that you're worried about pulling your hook out and he's worried about manipulating his fish. So what you really have are two quite different fishing techniques. If you are playing a big bonefish on a #6 hook, and you bend your rod way around and the fish suddenly makes a run, there is so much friction on your line guides that you may break the leader. You're not pulling the hook out, you're breaking the leader. But if you get a #22 hook in a big, brown trout, your big problem is not breaking the leader, it's just pulling the hook out or . . .

DAVE WHITLOCK — Well, you're breaking the leader, too!

FLIP PALLOT — Well, what I am saying, Dave, is that if you want to beat a fish, you'd be better off doing it with a 2-foot rod than a 10-foot rod, in any configuration you place that rod in. And if breaking the leader then becomes a factor, then I suggest that that's a function of the drag or the way that you play the fish with your hands. But the short lever gives you the best mechanical advantage over the fish. The longer the lever, the more advantage the fish has, and that's physics.

LEFTY KREH — Well, actually, it doesn't work that way either. When you get into a strong fish on a light line with a real soft rod, the fish may not be able to break anything, but, of course, you can't do much with it either! Now we're talking about a long fight with a brown trout being 15 minutes. If you hook a tarpon on a real soft rod, you're going to be six hours, you see?

FLIP PALLOT — But I can't even conceive of fighting a trout for 15 minutes. I mean, we fight big tarpon for only 15 minutes. If you're really talking about fighting a fish, then the pressure you need is, or should be, a function of drag.

LEFTY KREH — Actually, I don't use much drag when I fight trout. I use my hand and the resistance on the guides for fighting big trout with small tippets.

DAN BLANTON — The problem is that we all are individuals, and we have different ways of dealing with our fish. What I was talking about with the striped bass, Flip, was a specialized situation, I suppose. There is no one way of doing things in this business. If the fish takes all the choices away from you — if it's going down rapids or going into pilings or into a weed bed — whatever line you're using, you have to stop that run! You only have two choices, turn it or lose it! And I believe, from my experience, that if you can keep the full bend in the rod so that it acts like a spring or a shock absorber, and you're totally committed to turning that fish and playing the angles, you have the best chance.

FLIP PALLOT — I disagree with that, I really do!

Dan BLANTON — I'm fishing right by the airport in San Francisco Bay, and a big 747 comes over, 20 feet above my head, and I lose all my concentration. And all of a sudden, a fish pulls my rod straight and boom! . . . it's gone, just like that! An instant break-off. It's over! But if I can keep the full bend in that rod, I'll land at least 90 percent of the fish I hook.

JIM TEENY — You're saying it's more forgiving?

DAN BLANTON — It's forgiving. It's a shock absorber. A fly rod is a shock absorber. When we set the hook on a light line, the tip gives, and this shock absorption forgives some mistakes.

LEFTY KREH — Really, I feel there are two fishing situations here. One is where you've got open water and you've got a fairly good-sized hook in the fish. In that situation, I agree with Flip.

But I also agree with what you guys are talking about, particularly on trout. I know from experience that when you've got a small confined area, where there are weed beds and rocks and stuff like that, if you place a deep bend in the rod, you can put constant pressure on the fish that in the end will pay off.

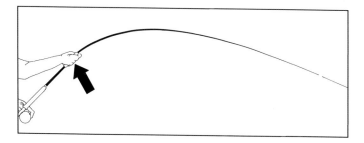

*Incorrect Rod Fighting Technique for Big Fish — When the angler grasps the rod this far from the handle, only the portion of the rod forward of his hand is bending and fighting the fish.*

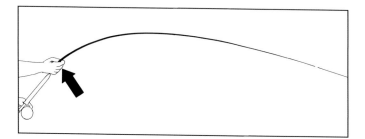

*Correct Rod Fighting Technique for Big Fish — But, when the angler grips the rod in this position, the strongest portion of the rod — the butt section — is brought into play and much more pressure can be exerted on the fish.*

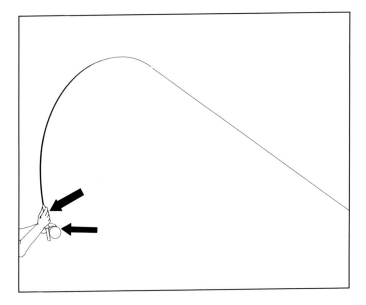

*Correct Rod Fighting Technique for Small Fish — When fighting trout or other smaller fish on fragile leaders, the spring of the rod is used to absorb any jolts on the line. The fingertips are pressed against the reel spool to deliver the desired drag pressure.*

*Are there major performance differences between standard two-piece rods and the new three and four-piece travel rods?*

DAVE WHITLOCK — I think that all the travel rods being made by the reputable rod manufacturers are wonderful fishing tools. It used to be — at least with the multiple-ferrule rods — that you could see a big difference in their weight and the way they performed. For some reason the manufacturers always seemed to put their cheapest materials on those rods. But I think today, the Loomis people, Orvis, Fisher, Scott and Sage, for example, they all do such a wonderful job ferruling those rods in multiple pieces that there's really absolutely no handicap to a three or four-piece travel rod.

I had just as soon fish with a three or four-piece rod as with a two-piece or even a one. Because, honest to God, after 10 minutes of casting, I can't tell a difference.

And the convenience of being able to put a rod in the overhead compartment of an airplane or in the back of your car without all that length is just super. I've got a case over here with three or four rods in it, and I've been carrying it on and off the airlines as a test thing. So, for example, when I arrived at the Yellowstone the other day, I was able to pull out a rod and fish with it almost immediately. How nice it is compared with what we used to have to do to get a personal rod to a destination.

If there is a disadvantage with the travel rods, it's probably the slight additional weight and a little additional cost. But for the modern fly fisherman, I don't think that either of those factors should stop him from equipping himself with the three or four-piece travel rods.

LEFTY KREH — You can hide them from your wife, too!

JOHN RANDOLPH — I agree with that. But I am particularly interested to hear what the saltwater guys have to say about three and four-piece rods in terms of breakage.

GARY BORGER — An interesting thing about four-piece rods is that sometimes they actually cast better than two-piece rods.

FLIP PALLOT — Hallelujah!

GARY BORGER — Because the ferrules add a little stiffness at different points along the rod. And there are some rod

OVERLEAF: *Steelhead flies.*

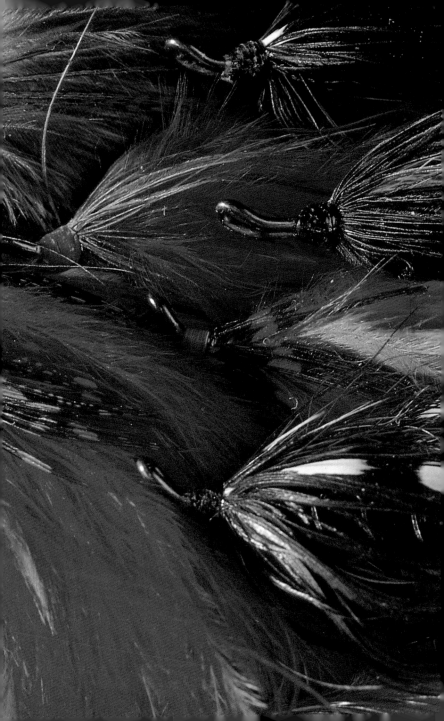

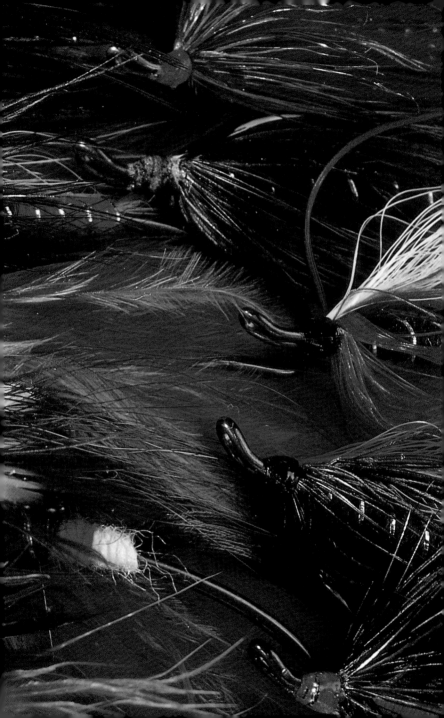

actions you cannot actually repeat in two-piece rods that you can achieve in a four-piece model. One of my very favorite rods is an 8-foot, four-piece, for a 5-weight line. It's a marvelous casting instrument.

LEFTY KREH — Oddly enough, the rod engineers say that they can make better rods out of three pieces than they can out of two pieces, because then they can move the ferrule out of the center of the rod.

There are several other things that people don't understand about multi-piece rods. One reason that they cost a little more is that the manufacturers have to make four individual rods, whereas in the case of the two-piece rod, they're just making two rods. Another thing is that at least one rod company I know of is today making its three-piece saltwater rods with a beefed-up butt section. And by having the versatility of making the rod in three sections, it can really contour these models so that the rods can get a lot more power in the back-end so that they cast better.

DAN BLANTON — I prefer four-piece rods over the three-piece models, only for one reason. When I reach my fishing destination, my rods are rigged and I'm ready to go. I see a lot of people who break down their equipment every night, then walk to the stream the next morning and have to re-assemble it. It's like a ritual. To me, it's wasting fishing time!

DAVE WHITLOCK — Amen! Amen!

DAN BLANTON — I've had fish on the bank before these other guys even had their leaders on. Because with a four-piece rod, I can break it down evenly and have two equal lengths of rod that I can stuff into my rod bag.

LEFTY KREH — You mean, you break it down, two pieces together and two pieces together?

DAN BLANTON — Two pieces together, lines strung, with the fly connected on the end. I can shove it down into a rod bag. With the three-piece models, since the pieces are uneven, I can't do that.

JIM TEENY — Well, there's not much to add there. I'm pro four-piece or three-piece.

FLIP PALLOT — I love the convenience. I really agree with Gary that many rod actions are enhanced by the ferrules. Provided that they are properly joined — and there's a correct procedure for doing that — I have never, ever had a ferrule failure with one of the modern, sleeve-type ferrules. I am not crazy about the spigot ferrules. But the Loomis and Sage-type ferrules, for example, I think are marvelous! Never had a failure. Never! I have never had a failure with a three or four-piece rod. And now I use them exclusively. What else can I say?

LEFTY KREH — There are two other points I'd like to make. The main reason why sleeve ferrules, the types where the female fits down over the male, come apart — and rod manufacturers are remiss in not telling the customer this — is that people put them together improperly. For example, if you have the butt section guide sitting straight up, and you put the tip section into the butt ferrule straight up so that the tip and butt guides are lined up exactly, and then shove them together, they may come apart.

What you want to do, instead, is to turn the tip section so that the tip guide is at a 90-degree angle from the butt guide, and then rotate the sections as you are shoving them together. If you do that, your ferrules will never loosen or come off.

And you need to lubricate the ferrules. I know Dan uses paraffin. I have used paraffin as well as beeswax, but beeswax picks up too much dirt, and paraffin doesn't seem to stay on a long time. But Russ Peak talked me into using ordinary candle wax. If you fish frequently, about once a year you ought to take a candle and rub it on the male ferrules. You can use most anything, I suppose . . . the point is to lubricate the thing.

The other thing I would like to point out is that most of the manufacturers of the multi-piece rod-carrying cases design them so that rods can be placed on board a plane. And that's fine. But I think that you ought to equip yourself with a carrying case that has an outside pouch or two where you can store reels, flies, leaders, pliers — all the essential things you need when you get to your destination, regardless of happens to the rest of your baggage.

DAVE WHITLOCK — See that bag right there on the floor? I want to show you that at the coffee break. Everything's there that you need to fish. I call it my fly-fishing insurance bag. Because everything that I need to fish for a week is in there, except some clothes. I may be fishing naked, but I'll be fishing!

*What makes a rod break?*

FLIP PALLOT — With graphite, from what I have been able to learn — and have really tried to learn something about it — there are only two reasons. First, you impact and fracture the rod somehow. You can even do that with a weighted fly.

The other thing is that you ruin the hoop strength of the blank with too much bending. The fibers of graphite go through a good deal of elongation on the top of the rod when you bend it, but they have to compress too. That's what happens to the bottom of the rod when you bend it. And you get no warning when the fibers decide to let go, as you do with glass or cane. No noise, no nothing! And suddenly . . .

LEFTY KREH — Well, glass will take four times more bending than graphite. And people don't realize that when your rod breaks under that kind of pressure, you're crushing the fibers and the rod is breaking on the inside.

JOHN RANDOLPH — Okay, but what kind of behavior leads to that? Improper behavior?

FLIP PALLOT — A vertical rod position is one way to do it. I mean, when you take a vertical rod position and tilt the rod way back behind you and strike the fish.

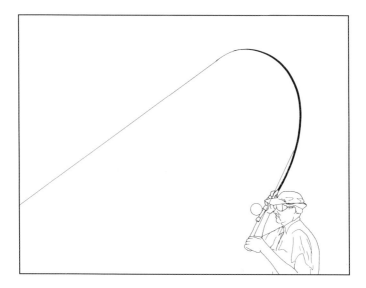

*Too Much Rod Bend*

DAVE WHITLOCK — The term we used to use for that was "high sticking."

LEFTY KREH — In a striking or fighting position, if you bring the handle of the rod more than 50 to 60 degrees back from the fish, or in other words, you go 90 degrees or even further back, you have a chance of breaking your rod and losing your fish, too.

JIM TEENY — I'll tell you something I see all the time — and this has to do with safety as well as rod breakage. I see people fishing with split shot or a heavily weighted fly who will get the hook snagged up in the bush behind them, at which point they'll jerk their rod back and forth to break it loose, or even pull straight back. And, boy, if that sucker comes off and it comes back, Bam! It's right to their rod tip or even their eye! Because there is a tremendous amount of stretch in that line.

The better and safer way to try to get unhooked, I always tell them, is to strip out some additional line, then reach out in front of the rod tip and grab the line with your hands and pull directly on the line, turning your body and pulling away from your face. That releases all tension on the rod, and you don't have to worry about breaking it. But don't pull straight back! If that hook breaks free, it's just like a bullet shooting back! Turn and pull to the left or the right, so that if that fly does break loose, it's going to fly back off to the side.

GARY BORGER — Let me just tell you a little story about that. It's amusing because it happened to somebody who was snagging salmon! And I clapped!

These guys were snagging big Kings that were running into the mouth of the Oconto River, using heavy spinning rods with 50-pound test monofilament and spoons with huge treble hooks. Now the law there says you cannot use a hook with a gap of more than 1/2-inch, so to get around that they were putting lead on their hooks to fill up the gap. Then when they would cast a spoon out, it would go right to the bottom, and they would snag Kings and just jerk them in.

Well, this guy got his rig hung up on the bottom. He was jerking and pulling on it, jerking and pulling on it — and it wouldn't come loose. So he did the same thing you were talking about, Jim. He just held the rod and backed up, and kept backing up and backing up. And all of a sudden that big hook came loose and the spoon came zinging out of the water and hit him on the shin. It sounded like a rifle shot when it hit him! Knocked him flat and he was screaming and howling and rolling. And everybody was cheering! Wonderful!

JOHN RANDOLPH — That's great!

FLIP PALLOT — You know, there is another item of behavior that causes graphite rods to break. I see this a lot, too. Somebody will be fighting a fish and suddenly they'll reach up with their other hand and grab the rod and try to put extra pressure on the fish by bringing the tip into the game. That's another kiss of death.

LEFTY KREH — I do consulting work for one of the larger rod companies, and what they have found is that there are two ways in which many modern graphite rods break.

One way is when people are traveling in a boat — a drift boat or a flats boat, or whatever. They'll set their rod down on a sharp edge, like a boat seat, and it will vibrate as the boat is moving, sometimes producing a minute fracture in the rod. And if you get the tiniest fracture on the surface of a graphite rod, you stand a good chance of losing it.

The other way people break rods all the time — the one the manufacturers hear about the most — is people hitting their rods with weighted streamers or nymphs.

JIM TEENY — I broke my first rod in Alaska that way.

LEFTY KREH — What happens is that when you pull back on the line to bring the fly out of the water, the energy created from the release of surface tension on a weighted fly even as small as a #14 nymph is so powerful that it can fracture the outside of a graphite rod. People are blaming good rod companies for this, but it's a very unfair accusation. It's not the manufacturer's fault.

DAN BLANTON — About that rod vibration problem. Nowadays most of the good skiffs I fish in have tubes that you can store your rods in while you're moving. But I think a much better way is to use the soft padded reel and rod bags that everybody's selling these days. These bags protect the rods from the effects of vibration as well as keep the sun off. In some models you can even store three or four rods at one time. They are a good travel item.

LEFTY KREH — People don't really realize how susceptible graphite rods are to sharp edge hitting.

DAN BLANTON — There is another place where I have seen fishing rods broken. I've witnessed this in my fly-fishing schools. Students will often drop a fly rod. When they're taking the rod apart, they'll drop the butt of the rod so that the tip end of the butt section hits the concrete. And when that happens, you can get linear fractures along the length of the rod. It's almost as if the ferrule end has been crushed a little bit. But even though it hasn't really been crushed, because it's been hit going straight down, fracture lines develop. So, then they rig the rod back up again, and while they're casting, all of the sudden the rod will break off right at the ferrule. When I see that happen, I always know exactly why. Again, the rod has been dropped so that the tip end of the butt section has been hit and consequently gets fractured. So that's another type of situation where you have to be careful.

LEFTY KREH — And the manufacturers are taking a rap on that, too. The same type of thing used to happen with fly lines. It used to be — I don't know how it is now — but years ago, when I used to do consulting work for Scientific Anglers, they had a policy that if a person returned a fly line that had ring checks — little round splits in the first 10 feet of the line — they would send him a replacement line without any argument. But they kept a log of these returns. And if the same person sent back the replacement line, they would just give him a full refund and tell him to buy somebody else's line instead.

What was happening was that as these people were casting, they were making wide loops and then at the end accelerating forward too fast, taking the line back around a curve as they came forward and literally pulling the vinyl on the line apart. And yet you couldn't tell your customer that he was a bad caster, because you'd make an enemy that way! You just had to hope he would go buy somebody else's line. And today, the same type of thing is going on with rods. Almost all of the broken rods that go back to manufacturers are the fault of the fly fisherman.

*Regarding matching rod weight to line weight, while it's true that rod manufacturers specify the line weights that should be used with each of their rods, are there some fishing situations where a lighter or heavier line weight should be used?*

DAVE WHITLOCK — I'll take the first shot at this. Sometimes I get psyched out whenever I'm going to run down to the river, and I pick up a 6-weight rod and can't find a 6-weight line. It's so ridiculous, because a lot of times a 5 or 7-weight line would have worked just as well for the kind of fishing I was planning to do. Exact rod and line matching doesn't make much difference in a lot of situations. But still, for an inexperienced fly fisherman, who really doesn't yet have a feel for balancing his cast by adjusting his rod motion to the amount of line he has outside the tip on the cast, the manufacturers' line-weight guidelines are useful.

LEFTY KREH — You mean the line designations that are printed on the fly rod?

DAVE WHITLOCK — Yes. Because then at least the person is in the ballpark with what he's fishing. I have always tried to impress on people that there is an enormous difference, on a 6-weight rod, for example, between having out 20 feet of line versus 80 feet. I think that as they begin to fly fish, people need to understand more about that.

I think that a skillful fly fisherman should be able to take a rod and use several different line weights — either lighter or heavier — and achieve the casting performance he wants. For example, a person who recognizes that he has rather slow reflexes might want to overload his rod a little bit more, just to soften the rod or get more flex. Or a lot of times when people are having problems with slowing down the drift on their forward cast, if they would go to a line that was one weight lighter, it wouldn't shock the rod as much. So there are many ways we can use line weights above or below what the rod is primarily designed for.

JOHN RANDOLPH— And, you know, sometimes the problem can be with the rod manufacturers. I remember one manufacturer was putting out a new 3-weight rod. They wanted to call the rod a "Western 3" so they put more beef in it for faster action, but it was actually a 5-weight! And a lot of the new travel rods that are made in three and four sections can be stiffer than normal because of the extra ferrules, so their line designations can be off the mark. So as a general rule, if the rod doesn't feel right to you, try some different line weights on it and see if it feels right. Say it's rated for 5-weight and the tip seems to be a little fast. Just go up to a 6 or even a 7-weight line. Or let's say you're in a fishing situation where you're using a 3-weight rod with a 3-weight line and you want to load the rod to fish up close. Just add a line weight — go to a 4 or even a 5-weight line. You've really got to do a lot of experimenting these days, because even though the manufacturers set a design standard based upon their engineering research and field testing, they don't always get it right, in addition to which there's a lot of variability subjectively between fly fishermen.

LEFTY KREH — Well, it can come from variability in the rod manufacturing process too, John. When they cut the cloth, they've got all these lines of graphite lying on the cloth and they put the template down and then cut. If they happen to compress the graphite a little bit, you can get a rod that will cast a line size heavier, and if they happen to spread the graphite a little bit, it's just the opposite result. We're all human. I would be willing to bet that if you took 20 rods from any top-line manufacturer, all designated as 6-weight, there would probably be at least one 5-weight rod and one 7-weight rod in the batch. The rod manufacturers will tell you that.

GARY BORGER — I think for the beginning angler, the most important rule to remember is that if you consistently fish short lines, under 30 feet, go a line weight heavier than the manufacturer calls for. And if you consistently fish lines longer than the standard 30 feet, go a line weight lighter, because you're aerializing more line, which means there's more line weight line outside the rod tip.

I have also noticed that people who cast well generally tend to use a line weight lighter than the manufacturer calls for. Not necessarily because they are casting longer distances, but because they have such a fast casting stroke. Because their timing is very, very precise. As a consequence they can load the rod with less line weight than is required for the average angler.

LEFTY KREH — If I'm making a lot of long casts on windy days, I go one line size lighter and extend about another 15 feet of line. From the standpoint of the weight ratio between my rod and line, that puts me back to where I would normally be on a calm day. But now I've got 15 more feet of line outside the rod tip already going toward the target, so I can cut down on the amount of line I need to shoot. And I've got a thinner line. But most people will go just the opposite way.

DAVE WHITLOCK — Just the opposite! I've noticed that too.

LEFTY KREH — Let's say you're using an 8-weight line and you want to throw long casts. If you go down to a 7-weight and extend extra line beyond the rod tip — and incidentally, this is not theory, this is what every major tournament caster in Europe and the U.S. does — if you add more length of line outside the rod tip, you add more weight. And then you are also throwing a thinner line, and you can throw it farther.

If you do just the opposite, and go to a heavier line for casting long distances in windy conditions, not only is the diameter of the heavier line larger, but what really is critical is that as a result of that heavier weight out there, you may start bending your rod in longer bows and start making bigger loops.

But as Gary says, a heavier line is the right choice for short range casting. Fly casting at short range in Argentina and New Zealand are good examples of this. Frequently in New Zealand and Argentina you can get a lot of wind. Or a lot of times out in the Rockies the wind picks up considerably in the afternoon. When I encounter winds like this, if I have been fishing drys on a 4-weight rod, for example, I'll switch to a 5-weight line. I'm fishing short distances with maybe only 10, 12, or 15 feet of line out anyway, and I can load my line so much better with the heavier line.

But I think the most important thing we need to recognize about this subject is demonstrated by this story. Just the other day when I was putting on a demonstration at a tackle show, a guy came up to me and said, "I can't cast this rod because I don't think it has got the right line size." He was holding a 7-weight rod. And I told him, "Go inside and ask them if they'll loan us a 3, 4, 5, 6, 8, 9, 10, and 11-weight line." He brought out all these lines, and I cast each one of them just fine on his 7-weight rod! Because by using a longer casting stroke, with a short acceleration — as I advocate in the modern fly casting method that I teach — an experienced caster should be able to cast five or six different line sizes on almost any good graphite rod being manufactured today.

Now I know the rod manufacturers are not particularly happy about this for an obvious reason. But anybody in this room — or any experienced fly caster, for that matter

— can easily cast at least five different line sizes on almost any good graphite rod in the mid-range size, from 6 to 9-weight.

DAN BLANTON — I was just about to say, Lefty, that any good caster can handle lines through a broad range of weights with any good rod.

I also agree with you, up to a point, about reducing line size in the wind. But for me, it also depends on the size of the fly. What I do, if I need heavier line in the wind to carry the same size fly, I just make sure the outfit is balanced. I wouldn't try to put a 13-weight line on a 10 or 11-weight rod. I would fish the line the rod was designed for, because sometimes the fly size just won't permit you to go down to a lighter weight. It just won't work.

The other thing about this is in reference to using shooting heads. As I understand it, in their rod engineering, the manufacturers generally try to achieve a design that will yield balance and optimum performance for the average caster with about 30 feet of line extended beyond the rod tip. Consequently, when using shooting heads, if you just went along with the manufacturer's specification, some of the graphite rods — particularly those with the higher modulus, or stiffer rods, or whatever you want to call them — don't necessarily reach their maximum performance. You see, you only have 30 feet of line out, and any overhang of shooting head and line that you extend beyond the tip may not load the rod to its optimum performance, particularly with big flies. So I generally recommend that when you buy a system of shooting heads, you select them in a weight that is one line heavier than your rod calls for. And for some rods, even two weights heavier. But at least one weight heavier and you'll be in the ballpark.

LEFTY KREH — Danny, every guy I know that really knows a lot about shooting heads uses at least one size heavier than what his rod calls for.

DAN BLANTON — And most rods will handle from two to three or even four weights heavier if you know how to lob cast a little bit.

LEFTY KREH — Don't you find, Danny, that the faster the sink rate of the line, the heavier that you can go . . .

DAN BLANTON — Because of the narrower diameter. It's diameter! Right!

LEFTY KREH — I'm really not sure why, but if I'm casting a an 8-weight rod, I can go to 9-weight with a floating line. But if it's a Deep Water Express sinking line, I can go up to a 10 or even an 11-weight.

DAN BLANTON — Well, Lefty, I really believe it is the difference between the diameter of a floating line versus a sinking line. Even though they weigh exactly the same, a floater, being many times greater in diameter than a sinker, requires more rod power to generate line speed and then maintain it. Plus the factor that floating lines are extremely air-resistant.

A sinker requires far less rod power because it is considerably smaller in diameter, cutting through the air like a knife. It is also denser. That's why you can overload your rod by as much as two or three line sizes when using sinking lines, particularly when using shooting heads. On the other hand, you can only barely manage one line size over when using a floater.

JIM TEENY — In the old days when they made a rod they didn't put the line size on it. And now I think that you could take almost any given rod and throw, like you said, three weights on it easy! Easy! So I think the whole theory of line size and rod weights matching came about when the manufacturers figured out they could sell more rods and lines that way!

LEFTY KREH — Well, no, I don't think they did it with that in mind. I think it was mainly to make available a variety of rods and lines to make sure that the average guy had the tools to get him in the ballpark for all kinds of fly fishing. I don't really think they did it for that. Not many people can handle a fly rod like you can, Jimmy!

FLIP PALLOT — The approach that I take to this problem more than anything else now — just because it's so much simpler and there are so many new tapers in fly lines today, particularly in the saltwater lines — is that it really gets down to what Gary said before, and that's how far away do you plan to be fishing? What length cast are you going to be dealing with?

So rather than changing line sizes all the time, what I'm doing instead is simply changing tapers — saltwater, bonefish, bass, tarpon, steelhead, weight-forward, or what have you. You know, with all the special tapers they are making today, if you're using one of the better graphite rods, you don't need to change line sizes, just go to the different tapers. So that's the way I go, rather than changing line sizes.

LEFTY KREH — That's a good point, Flip. But one of the things we really do need in the tackle industry is a standardization among manufacturers regarding the densities and sinking rates of underwater lines, a common system that everybody could easily understand.

DAN BLANTON — Well, they are trying to standardize. But the competition to achieve faster sinking lines prohibits the tackle manufacturers from working together on that, I think. Scientific Anglers wants to have the fastest sinking line and Cortland wants to have the fastest sinking line, and Orvis wants to have the fastest sinking line, and they keep these things secret from each other.

LEFTY KREH — That's a problem! But getting back to rods, despite what we've had to say here, I think that people who are not as skilled at casting as we are shouldn't deviate too much from the line-weight classifications that the manufacturers recommend. The top rod companies — Sage and Loomis and Orvis and Winston, for example — have put a lot of engineering time into developing some really very precise tools for modern fly fishing. So if he buys a rod from a reputable manufacturer that recommends the use of a specific line weight, the unskilled or even the average caster is not going to do nearly as well with a line size heavier or lighter.

OVERLEAF: *Steelhead tackle, Olympic Peninsula, Washington.*

CHAPTER TWO

# REELS

*Is a direct-drive reel better than an anti-reverse model?*
*Are there situations where one is superior to the other?*
*What about saltwater applications?*

FLIP PALLOT — It's going to come as a great surprise to everybody, but I really think direct-drive reels are better fish-fighting tools. They are lighter and more reliable, but mainly, they are better fish-fighting tools.

JIM TEENY — I think for steelhead and trout and everything that I fish for, direct-drive is very adequate, but I am quick enough to get my fingers out of the way. That's the real key to deciding which kind of reel to use. A direct-drive reel can be a real knuckle-buster. If people are going to be clumsy or stick their hand in there by accident, it can really hurt. And it can also break a fish off. And if you are fighting a big fish while wearing heavy clothes — maybe a raincoat or a sweater plus a vest — and have your rod butt jammed against your chest, if the fish starts a run and your handle has to turn, you may get it caught in a sleeve or something. Also, some of the anti-reverse models are heavier. But I think both kinds of reel drives are fine. I suppose it ends up being really just a matter of personal preference.

LEFTY KREH — You didn't say it, Flip, but I'll bet you prefer the direct-drive because every time you turn the handle, you know you're recovering line. We want to make sure that everybody understands that.

JIM TEENY — Yeah, that is a positive aspect. Every time you do a turn on a direct-drive reel, you know without question that you are gathering line. Sometimes I have seen people with anti-reverse reels just winding and winding and not gaining line.

DAN BLANTON — Since I use anti-reverse reels for big game as well as small, I would not agree that direct-drive is the only reel to use, for at least a couple of reasons. From the standpoint of weight, as least in the big game models, anti-reverse reels weigh about the same as direct-drives.

Regarding line recovery, while that's a valid point, I think the problem really applies only when you are using an anti-reverse reel with the light tippet classes — when you have to play a light drag, using tippets of 8 pounds to 6 pounds and below. But on big game with heavier tippets, I apply a very firm drag. I believe if the fish is going to take line — whether it's one yard or 100 yards — it's going to have to earn every inch of it. So I play it pretty close to the wire when it comes to drag. I really do play a hard drag. So I don't have a problem picking up line.

Also, I believe that when you fight a fish, when you gain line, you first gain it by using the rod. You pump the rod up using short strokes, and then reel down quickly to gain line. And if you have a problem with slippage when pumping up, you palm the rim. There are some anti-reverse reels being manufactured today that have palming rims, too. So with the exception of these light-line applications, I see no problems with the anti-reverse.

The other reason I sometimes like an anti-reverse reel is that I do a lot of King salmon fishing from a pram, a boat. And when I hook a fish, I've got to reach back, pull up the bow anchor, pull up the stern anchor, stuff the rod between my legs or under my arm, and row away from a line-up of boats. And in making all these moves, I've had a whirling handle from a direct-drive reel catch in my sleeve or bang against something, and I've lost the fish.

There's also an aspect that applies to beginners, or to people who only fish perhaps once or twice a year. They'll take a direct-drive reel to the Keys or the Bahamas, for example, and since they're not adept at dealing with the handle problem, they'll blow fish. But with an anti-reverse, even though they may sometimes be cranking and not recovering line, that's just inefficient, but it won't cost them a fish.

So for beginners, or if you're a surgeon or pianist who needs to worry about breaking his knuckles, I say get an anti-reverse. But if you're going to do a lot of fly fishing — with the exception of the clothing situation that Jim made a very good point about, or my specialized problem with a direct-drive reel handle in fishing from a pram — I would, like you guys, have to cast my final vote for the direct-drive.

LEFTY KREH — I think both type reels have valid applications. Speaking for myself, just like Dan, I believe I can fight big fish as well, or just about as well, with a slip clutch anti-reverse model, because I can control the fish with my hand on the rod. What I do is bring the rod up and only wind as I come down. Admittedly that takes a little more experience than a beginner may have. But again, just as Dan says, even if a beginner may sometimes be winding without recovering line and wasting his energy, at least he hasn't lost the fish. But once you become as skilled as somebody like Dan or Flip or Jim, you're definitely going to be able to control your fish better with a direct-drive reel.

One point I think is very important is that a lot of novice fly fishermen who are using a direct-drive will probably at first get their reel hand banged up pretty badly a couple of times. And then during the middle of a fight they will begin worrying about their hand instead of the fish.

Also, I think that any direct-drive reel should only have one handle. A reel with two handles just hits your knuckles twice as much, and you don't need that.

JIM TEENY — That's a Cuisinart!

LEFTY KREH — I also think the handle on a direct-drive reel should be constructed to be slightly smaller, so that it's easier to remove your hand from it quickly — as opposed to the handles on most anti-reverse reels which have those big, corrugated-shaped handles. On direct-drives, I want that smaller handle.

GARY BORGER — Well, I'll just say for trout fishing, direct-drive is really the only way to go, because you need the instantaneous control that it can give you. And you also benefit from the light weight. And of course, you don't need heavy drags with trout. I don't even use a drag on my reel. I just set it to zero.

JIM TEENY — You just need enough tension so the line doesn't override.

GARY BORGER — And even then, I take the drag completely off and just use my little finger against the rim to keep the line from overrunning. The less drag, the better.

*Should a right-handed fly fisherman equip himself with a left-hand-drive reel and wind with his weaker left hand? Or should he do just the opposite, equip himself with a right-hand-drive reel and wind with his dominant right hand?*

DAVE WHITLOCK — Well, I definitely feel that since you are going to be casting with your dominant hand, you ought to reel with your weaker hand. For example, if you are right-handed, you should reel with your left hand, and train your left hand to do the reeling. I don't think you should make the rod hand do all those reel movements, and I teach that method. I have had instructors on my staff who always switched hands, and I would require them to do it the other way, at least while they were teaching with me, because I really believe in that. And as I recall, without exception, nobody had any problem with it after a little while.

LEFTY KREH — Do you believe in that for saltwater and steelhead fishing, too?

DAVE WHITLOCK — I believe in it for all purposes, because I trained my weaker hand with exercise and fishing. It needs to be just as strong as my dominant hand.

LEFTY KREH — But how about the average guy?

DAVE WHITLOCK — It's still the same thing with the average guy, I think, because he's usually been doing some spin casting or bait casting. And he's learned to crank with his other hand pretty well.

JOHN RANDOLPH — I cast with my right hand, which is my dominant hand, and I crank the reel with my left hand. Not because I am concerned about switching the rod over to the other hand after I have a hook-up. I am not concerned about that. But when the fish takes the fly, I want my rod to be in my dominant right hand, and I can get along okay handling line with my left hand.

The reason I don't switch, the reason I want my left hand to be in charge of just the reeling work, is that my left hand is really stupid. I can't even write my name with it. But when it comes to playing a fish, I want my dominant hand, which has better motor skills, to help me react to whatever that fish is doing. I can feel, by the pressure on the fly rod, what the fish is doing at all times. I can move my dominant hand faster, so that when a fish makes a turn I can move the rod much more quickly to counter its moves. So I play the fish with my right, or dominant hand, and reel with my left. That's the way I recommend doing it.

DAN BLANTON — What I'm hearing here is mostly from trout fishermen who advocate playing the fish with your dominant hand and reeling with your weaker hand. I totally disagree with that. And I'm very adamant about it, not just for trout fishing but for all kinds of fishing.

LEFTY KREH — We just noticed that!

DAN BLANTON — Let's review some history. When they first started manufacturing fly reels, you couldn't buy one with a left-hand retrieve. They were all right-hand retrieve models. I asked Joe Brooks about this years ago, and he said it was primarily because most people were right-handed, and also because most people play trout by stripping line in with their left hand — they don't even play fish off the reel. And they wanted the smooth and handle-less left side of the reel to be opposite their stripping hand so that nothing could obstruct their stripping action.

But let's take a look at fly fishing for big game. Unless you're truly ambidextrous, you do everything from the time you are born with your dominant hand. There is no more sensitive part of your anatomy than the fingers of your dominant hand. And of course, the musculature of your dominant hand is better developed, so it's stronger. And for applying drag pressure to my reel spool on big fish, I want that dominant and sensitive and stronger hand at work. You guys think you can crank that reel handle with your weaker hand okay on a trout, but when you get into tarpon and billfish that have taken out 300 yards of line and you're into the fight for 45 minutes, everybody that I have ever seen cranking the handle with their weaker hand develops finger cramps so severe they can't even turn the reel!

LEFTY KREH — Not Dave!

DAN BLANTON — I'm not talking about a guy who's been doing it for 30 years! I'm talking about a guy who's getting into the field, who's learning, and maybe wants to make the transition to big game. I have never seen anybody that's been adept at cranking on big fish with his weaker hand.

Let me give you an example of another advantage you get with big fish by being set up so that you reel with your dominant hand. Assume you're right-handed, and you're using a reel with a right-hand wind. After the hook-up, still holding your rod in your right hand as you are clearing line with your left hand, your reel handle will be on the right side, completely out of the way. I have watched — I have even photographed this — and I'm sure Flip has seen it, too. If a right-hander is in that same situation with a left-hand wind reel, as he is clearing line it will frequently wrap around the handle, and the game is over!

But it's easy enough, after you have cleared all your line and it's on the reel, to switch your rod from your right to left hand. You can do it in a micro-second.

JIM TEENY — All right! I'm along with you. You see, I came from the school of Pflueger. My first fly reel was a . . .

LEFTY KREH — The school of Pflueger?

JIM TEENY — Pflueger! My first fly reel was a Pflueger Medalist.

LEFTY KREH — You know that reel kept the company alive for seven years! If they hadn't had the Pflueger reel, they would have gone out of business. It was the most popular fly reel in the world for a long time!

JIM TEENY — Well, I'm right-handed and after a hook-up and I've cleared line back onto the spool, I switch hands and reel with my right hand. And I have no problem with changing the rod over to my left hand. But I really think that a person should do what he is the most comfortable with.

LEFTY KREH — You are being a politician!

JIM TEENY — But it's true. If you are used to casting with your right hand and reeling with your left, and you're not having a problem with it, you have no reason to change!

LEFTY KREH — Flip, what do you think?

FLIP PALLOT — I think right-handed human beings should reel right-handed. For the same reasons Dan mentioned. Your dominant hand is more sensitive, faster, and stronger than your weaker or sub-dominant hand. When a bonefish makes a 100-yard run — and sometimes they do — you could be looking at having to make 200 or 300 turns of the handle to get that fish back. And then it could turn around and go off another 50 or 75 yards, and you're looking at another couple of hundred turns of the handle. Or try a sailfish where you have 500 turns to recover from the first run! So I want my strong hand to handle that action.

This gets back a little bit to what Gary and Dan were talking about earlier. I mean, Gary clearly fights the fish more with the rod than I do. I fight the fish with the reel. I hold the handle of the reel and kind of point the rod at the fish and pull. And I actually use very little drag in any fishing situation — ever! I don't care how big the fish is. I use almost no drag! Everything I do, almost, is with the reel handle. I'm not pumping with the rod. My left hand just sort of locks the rod, and the way that I pump is by rotating my body and reeling . . . rotating my body and reeling. I never pump with my arms, so I don't need the strength in my right arm or the sensitivity that you need when you're fighting a trout with 2-pound test leader.

JOHN RANDOLPH — I have to admit, when I am fishing the big game fish — the real brutes — that I do go to right-hand reeling. I have to admit that.

DAVE WHITLOCK — So what you're talking about is really two different situations, trout fishing versus big game salt-water fishing. But I'll bet over 95 percent of fly fishermen will never fish for big saltwater game!

LEFTY KREH — Yes, Dave, but more people than that fish in saltwater. And more people than that fish for salmon and steelhead and big trout. Or at least they hope they'll be fishing for big trout! I'm like Dan. I have never had a trout fisherman that fished saltwater with me for the first time that ended up liking to wind with his weaker hand. When you have a real strong fish that's going to require you to recover a lot of line — I don't care if it's a tarpon or a sailfish or a steelhead or a big trout — I have never known a right-hander — unless he's a guy that has been fly fishing for a long time like you guys have — an average angler, that could reel even nearly as well with his left hand.

As Dave pointed out, a lot of them say to me, "Well, I spin cast all the time so I'm used to it." But the difference in spin casting and fly casting is that when you rotate a spinning reel, you rotate the reel handle around a large arc and that's easy to do with your weaker hand. But when you switch to a fly reel, you're generally working on a smaller arc, and it's much more difficult to make that thing go in a perfect circle with your weaker hand.

And the other thing is, people say, "Well, I've got to switch the rod to my other hand, and I may lose the fish." But when a fish is running 100 or 125 yards away, you have plenty of time to switch hands.

DAN BLANTON — But I don't do what Flip does. I don't hold the handle. I either palm the rim or grip the line against the rod. Then I pull the fish, because I'm afraid that if I'm holding onto the handle when I'm pulling, if the fish makes a tremendous surge while I'm trying to pull and I haven't connected yet, I'll lose it.

JIM TEENY — I use drag tension on the reel. I do. And I've noticed that most of you guys don't, but I do.

LEFTY KREH — Oh, I fly fish for big tarpon with less than a pound of drag.

JIM TEENY — Do you? I don't know why I have gotten into it, but I depend on the drag.

JOHN RANDOLPH — Why do you, Lefty?

LEFTY KREH — Because if I only have about a pound of drag, I can fight the fish just like Flip does. I bring my arms back and do short pumps with my reel handle. And the instant a fish surges away, I just let go of the handle . . .

JOHN RANDOLPH — Okay! Are you holding the reel?

LEFTY KREH — No, I'm holding the handle! I hold the handle and recover line with my body. There's not much arm movement. You're actually fighting with your legs and your back. But the big thing is that the instant the fish changes direction — and this is true whether you're fighting a four-pound brown trout or a 100-pound tarpon — you don't

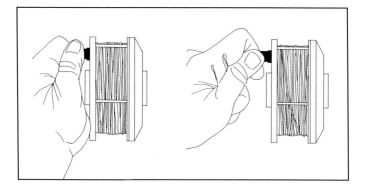

*Methods of Grasping Handle on Direct-Drive Reels — At left is shown incorrect method, angler is grasping the entire reel handle and cannot remove his hand quickly if fish surges. At right is shown the correct method, using only the fingertips.*

want to jerk on the leader. As soon as the fish goes the other way, you want to get any tension off that line . . .

FLIP PALLOT — That's where this whole bugaboo started about getting your hand out of the way of the handle. If you grasp the entire reel handle, the way most people do, then you're going to have a problem letting go of the handle and getting your hand out of way of the line when a fish surges. But if you will just hold the handle with your fingertips, then when the fish surges, allow the handle to just slip out of your fingertips . . .

LEFTY KREH — Your hand is out of the way before you . . .

FLIP PALLOT — Your hand is staying right where it was. You haven't gotten your hand out of the way of the reel, you've gotten the reel out of the way of your hand.

OVERLEAF: *Fly fishing the Umpqua River, Oregon.*

# CHAPTER THREE

# LINES

*What lines do you need for most situations in fresh and saltwater fly fishing?*

LEFTY KREH — What we're after here is what the average fly fisherman needs to know. What does he need in his bag when he goes fishing? We don't want him buying 25 or 30 lines. But on the other hand, to give you an example, one thing that I notice a lot, particularly on foreign trips, is that many fishermen just bring floating lines. And as a result, they're not equipped for many situations. That's the issue I'd like to discuss in detail.

JOHN RANDOLPH — Okay, good! Because one thing that Howard West at Scientific Anglers said to me once was, "Look, it's my complaint to you as an editor that you're not relating in your articles that the lines you take with you are just as important as the rods and the flies, because the lines deliver the fly under the particular fishing situation, and that's important."

For instance, I'm salmon fishing in Alaska. And a guy standing next to me is fishing on the surface and not catching fish, but I'm catching one fish right after another because I'm fishing the fly on the bottom. And I finally feel like I have to give him a break and lend him my tackle, because he has come to Alaska, as Lefty said, with only a floating line. If we're talking about presentation of the fly where the fish expects to see it, in whatever fishing environment we're in, from stillwater to moving water, all the way through — we're going to have a lot to talk about.

LEFTY KREH — Yes, we could spend the whole day on that! Dave, what do you say?

DAVE WHITLOCK — Well, what I'm always trying to do with our students is to cover why the line is so important in casting and presentation of the fly, and that the selection of fly lines — floating, sink-tips, and the other densities — is critically important in getting the fly to where the fish are.

I suppose that most people use floating lines because they are a little easier to cast, or we have made floating-line technique easier for people to understand. We start beginners out with floating lines, rather than sinking lines. But perhaps if we started a beginner out with a sinking line, he might be able to cast that sinking line just as well. A lot of people find that the floating line is more comfortable to use because that's what they started out with, and if they're good at it, if they can cast a long leader and a heavily weighted fly, they can get quite a range of depths with a floating line, from the surface right on down to 10 or 15 feet deep. So, a lot of people feel like they can get by with a floating line in most situations.

But looking at the other lines — for a example a sink-tip is probably the second most versatile line, in the sense that you can take flies on down to the lower depths and still have available some of the handling characteristics of a floating line, particularly the ease with which you can pick it up off the surface of the water. And then, of course, a full-sinking line is important for getting a fly real deep.

But frequently with the mind-fix of most beginning fly fishermen, they start getting into trouble as soon as the line begins to sink to any depth, because they don't know how to handle it. So most of them prefer the floating line because that keeps it in their ballpark. And, I think all of us are a little bit lax in training people at the beginner levels to understand how to select and use these other lines. We tell them that fly line selection is so important, particularly in regard to the presentation of the fly in various depths of water, but we don't practice what we preach. We just continue to stick a floating line in their hands and for the first six months or a year, they just fish with that. You can't blame them. That's what we taught them!

GARY BORGER— A line is a part of the presentation tactic that you're using, so you really have to consider what you want to do before you consider how to select a line. For example, if I want to fish giant midge larvae imitations in the Kamloops District, and I am fishing down 15 feet, I am *not* fishing with a sinking line! I'm fishing with a floating line and a 25-foot leader because I want the pupae to go back to the surface. I fish snail patterns and lakes a lot of times with floating lines and 25-foot leaders. I cast out over the sunken weeds and let the fly sink down so that the fish can pick it up as it's coming down. If I used a sinking line, it would put my fly right into the weeds on the bottom.

On the other hand, you may be fishing in only a foot and a half of water and need to use a sinking line instead of a floating line. Down on Silver Creek in Idaho, for example, there are some of the toughest fish you'll ever fish to. Those fish have been conditioned by so many fishermen using floating lines to the fact that if the fly is sinking or is going up towards the surface, they are going to get their lips ripped off if they take it. Those fish will *only* take a fly that's moving along the bottom. So on this water, even at a depth of only a foot and a half, you have to use a sinking fly line. So it is very important to really think about the whole presentation concept before you select your fly line.

LEFTY KREH — But for the average guy, what do you think he should have?

GARY BORGER — 90 percent of the time, a floating line.

LEFTY KREH — And the other 10 percent?

GARY BORGER — In lakes, a full-sinking line and in streams, a sink-tip.

LEFTY KREH — I basically agree with you.

DAN BLANTON — Oh, I do, too. I agree that any beginner would have to have a floating line and a sink-tip. I would also add a full-sinking line, maybe a #2 density. I think it is important to understand that in streams the fish are either on top or down deep. There are not too many times when they are right in the middle of the water column.

In lakes, however, it's a different story altogether. In lake fishing, the fish move up and down the water column according to the availability of food, which is often influenced by light intensity. Early in the morning fish are higher in the water column because that's where plankton and the bait-fish are. But as the light becomes more intense, fish move down. So you need to understand that in order to be effective in all situations, you need to be able to cover the entire water column.

And also, I think you need to take it further. If you want to be an advanced fly fisherman that can cover all the bases, I really believe that you need your standard lines — floating, sink-tip, and full-sinking — but also, you have to have shooting heads. Lefty knows that I am a strong advocate of shooting heads. I think any fly fisherman who does not learn how to use a shooting head, which is a distance line that can come in a lot of different densities and sink rates, has severely limited his angling horizons. Shooting heads have all kinds of applications in saltwater, freshwater, streams, rivers, lakes — any kind of water! And they are relatively easy to use and easy to accumulate. You can accumulate a whole system of shooting lines that will take you through all the available densities — there are just five or six —- without spending a lot of money. And they travel well. You can take them in a small package anywhere.

JIM TEENY — Well, I agree with Dan on the floating, sink-tip, and sinking lines, but I don't think it's emphasized enough, you know, why we need all these types of lines. It's because the fish feed at different levels. What is it . . . 90 to 95 percent sub-surface?

LEFTY KREH — I think it's about 90 percent.

JIM TEENY — Okay, so with that simple little thing in mind, when you can get fish to come to the surface, it's a joy. But if they're not coming up, and you can't get your fly down to the fish, that's when you're going to have your fishless days. That's where you definitely need to have a variety of lines to be ready to adapt to a situation right away. Because the quicker the angler can notice that what he's doing isn't working and make a line change, the better fly fisherman he's going to be.

FLIP PALLOT — In saltwater, I think most of the fishing is going to be done with just a regular floating line, and probably some of the newer specialized floating tapers that are being developed.

DAVE WHITLOCK — It's interesting that you say that, Flip, because Lefty just said about 90 percent of the fish feed under the surface of the water. Well, in saltwater, you can sometimes have as much depth as 1,000 feet, yet you still recommend a floating line, which shows that the floating line is really very versatile.

JOHN RANDOLPH — We need to clarify that . . .

FLIP PALLOT — The floating line is the basic saltwater line 90 percent of the time. Occasionally there will be situations where you need a neutral density line or a line that just sinks slightly, like an Intermediate line. And also — and I couldn't agree more with Dan about this — if you fail to use a system of shooting heads in saltwater, you're knocking off a lot of fun and a lot of neat fishing situations, as well. But with those three rigs — a floating line, an Intermediate line, and a system of shooting heads, I think you can get through all saltwater situations.

*Regarding sinking lines, from the large number
of designs now available, what are your
favorite selections and their use?*

LEFTY KREH — What I would like to do on this question would be for us to give some examples of various fishing situations where we would choose different sinking lines. I think that the people who are advancing beyond the beginning or average level of fly fishing and who are on their way to becoming advanced fly fishermen, would be real interested in this. Like, if you're fishing in a basin for tarpon, and there's a lot of floating grass, if you use a floating line, the grass catches the line and shunts down onto the fly and destroys your whole presentation. So you need to use a Monocore or Intermediate line or something like that instead, because when a line of this type hits the grass, it will slide off and sink below the grass, so that you can often fish through an entire area of floating grass with a clean fly.

Or, for example, take the uniform-sinking line, which has become one of my favorites of all sinking fly lines.

And then, of course, in that category of lines, there's Jim's Teeny Nymph line. I know we have made it a general rule for the Symposium not to mention specific manufacturers. But this is something special. I think that if we feel that if a particular manufacturer is doing something that nobody else is doing, or doing something better than anybody else, we should mention it. Because that's an obligation we have to our readers. And also, maybe that will encourage other tackle companies to create better products.

Jim, your line is one of the most versatile sub-surface lines I have ever seen. Why don't you just tell us a little bit about the line and why you use it?

JIM TEENY — Well, what uniform sink — which is really fairly new terminology — means is that the line sinks evenly. In the T-series of Teeny Nymph lines, which are designated T-130, 200, 300, 400, and 500, there's no taper in the sinking portion. You know, from the beginning of the sinking portion of the line to the tip it's all level, which means that it will sink uniformly throughout that length.

LEFTY KREH — Well, how does that vary from how a normal sinking line sinks?

JIM TEENY — Well, a lot of times with a tapered sinking line you get what I call "tip lag." After you make your cast and the line swing begins, the high density rear portion of the line is sinking down deep where the fish are, but the tapered tip portion is riding higher in water.

LEFTY KREH — So your tippet and fly are going to be several feet higher in your water column than the rest of your sinking line, way above the fish!

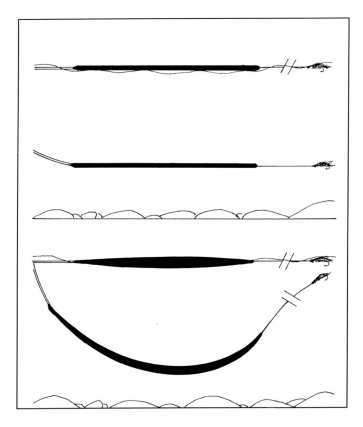

*Sinking Line Profiles: Uniform (top) and Tapered (bottom)*

JIM TEENY — At times, it can absolutely do that!

LEFTY KREH — And so, tell them about your line.

JIM TEENY — Well, what it is, it's a level shooting or running line attached to a section of Deep Water Express sinking line from 24 to 30 feet long, depending on the weight. It's all one piece and there's no . . .

LEFTY KREH — It's all level, too, isn't it?

JIM TEENY — It's all level, both sections are level. But they are perfectly balanced. They roll cast and false cast really nicely. And there is no splice or hinge at the connection point. Also, they are color-coded so the running line is a certain color, and all the sinking sections are dark to decrease their visibility under water. This color coding gives you a clear indication of how much of your line is underwater, so you can gauge when to pick it up for the next cast. This gives the angler better line control than a uniform-sinking line which is colored the same way throughout its length. What it does for the average angler, I think, is that it helps take away some of the guesswork about when he should pick up his line. And that also actually helps most people cast a little greater distance with less effort.

LEFTY KREH — In effect, what you have is a shooting head?

JIM TEENY — Yes!

LEFTY KREH — But it casts almost like a regular weight-forward line, wouldn't you say that?

JIM TEENY — Yes, probably in a way . . .

LEFTY KREH — As far as the casting mechanics, not the fishing part. It goes faster.

JIM TEENY — It does go faster, but with a bigger loop. You don't cast a tight loop with one of these lines, because if you try to overpower the cast, you get a real mess!

LEFTY KREH — I think it's one of the finest sinking lines you can use. You call them "T" lines, right?

JIM TEENY — T-Series, yeah, thank you.

LEFTY KREH — And there's a T-300, which is for what? And, you've got a 200, a 300, a 400 . . .

JIM TEENY — Well, as I've mentioned, we have a 130, a 200, a 300, a 400, and a 500, plus a line I call a Mini-tip.

LEFTY KREH — And how do you differentiate between those numbers?

JIM TEENY — We break it down like this: the 130 works on rods designed for 4, 5, and 6-weight lines; the 200 works on rods designed for 5, 6, 7, and even 8-weight lines. The 300 works on 8, 9, and 10-weight rods, and the 400 and 500s are designed for use with heavy rods of 9-weight or higher where you want very high rates of sink.

FLIP PALLOT — Are these numbers grain weights?

JIM TEENY — Yes. It's the grain weight of the front section, which is 24 feet or longer depending on the weight, so that when you get up to the 400, the density is higher than even lead core. People are even using the 500 now to catch halibut. I mean, it just goes right down!

JOHN RANDOLPH — I'd like to explain something about those Teeny lines. Reading the water is important in using them. In other words, the speed of the water and the depth of the water. So that you walk up to heavy, deep water and you say, "That's 400 water." Or you walk up and it's shallow water. You know, the speed of the current is slower, and you say "That's 200 water." And so on. And once you get in the habit of doing that, you can place your line down to any depth in the water column that you want, on any type of water, and present the fly just exactly where you think the fish are holding. They are terrific!

In Alaska, fishing to Pacific salmon, you've got to have your fly on the bottom or you're not fishing. I wouldn't go to Alaska without Jim's Teeny lines.

LEFTY KREH — I think they are fantastic. I guess I'm plugging your lines, Jim, but I feel they represent a breakthrough in fly fishing that people ought to know about.

Dan, can you talk a little bit about your contour lines? Dan makes a three-part line that fishes contours, and I would like him to just briefly explain it to you.

DAN BLANTON — Well, it's similar to what Jim has done with his Teeny lines, which are full length lines, aren't they?

JIM TEENY — Yes, they're 82 feet long.

DAN BLANTON — Okay. All of us out on the Pacific coast — specifically salmon and steelhead fishermen — have been using shooting tapers, which are essentially based upon the same principles that Jim is talking about with his lines. The first vinyl-coated shooting taper made was a #2 fast-sinking line, and from there, manufacturers began offering other sink rates as it became feasible to market them, from the floating shooting head, to an Intermediate — which is very important in tidewater — a #1 slow-sink, a #2 fast-sink, a #3 extra-fast (or HI-D, as it is commonly called), a #4 (or High Speed HI-D, as it is commonly called) and so forth. And you read the water to select the appropriate line the same way that John was discussing with Jim's Teeny lines.

The big advantage of using shooting tapers is that if I've only got one rod and reel, to start the day I may load my reel with backing, monofilament shooting line, and say, a floating shooting head. Then I'll stick coils of a few various densities of sinking shooting heads in my vest, and I'm prepared to fish any water I want all day long without having to pack more than one rod or extra spools. Let's say

OVERLEAF: *Barbara Lewis fly fishing for trout on the Firehole River, Yellowstone National Park, Wyoming.*

I hit a heavy, deep run, where I need a #4 High Speed HI-D or a #5 Deep Water Express. I fish that through. Then I move down the river to slower water where I decide I need a lighter line. At that point, I simply unloop the Deep Water Express shooting head, loop on a lighter shooting head, and within seconds, I'm back to fishing with a line of the right density and sink rate for that particular water. I can move through an entire stream with one rod and reel that way. That's one big advantage of shooting tapers.

The other advantage is distance. I can remember a situation in Alaska on a particular bend of a river we were fishing. The fish were holding at 90 to 100 feet, and I couldn't wade any closer. But by using a shooting head, I was the only person in my group that could reach those fish. Now I couldn't reach them every cast, because I had to get the perfect cast. But when I did reach them, I caught fish.

Now the contour lines that Lefty has mentioned. What's interesting about this discussion of uniform-sinking lines is that a lot of us who got into this type fishing a long time ago have been using uniform-sinking lines for years. But we just made our own and didn't give them a name.

What we were doing is what I used to call slot fishing, but Lefty told me that a lot of people didn't understand what slot fishing meant. So let's call it channel fishing. If you're fishing a small steelhead stream and there is a channel of deep water . . .

JOHN RANDOLPH — The bucket . . . you mean the bucket . . .

DAN BLANTON — The bucket, the slot, the channel . . .

LEFTY KREH — Channel works better for most people.

DAN BLANTON — It's referred to a lot of different ways. So, what you've got is a short stretch of water where fish are holding against a high bank in deep water. In this situation, you don't have to make a long cast. You maybe need to make only about a 40-foot cast. But because the fish are down about 10 feet deep, and you've got a sloping bar, and the current is slow, you need a #5 sinking line to really reach the fish. So you fish a #5 line, but by the time your leader has started to bring your fly through the pod of fish, your line has bellied into the sand bar. Your fly is dead, it isn't moving. And the fish won't eat it if it's not moving!

To solve this sort of problem, we started literally splicing our lines together. We would take a 10-foot-long section of floating line, maybe another seven to 10 feet of #3 fast-sinking line, and then maybe on the end of that we would add about four feet of High Speed HI-D. We might even have put a piece of lead core on the end of that. This special rig will drift nicely down through that slot, placing your fly at just the depth where you believe the fish are holding.

Jim's Teeny lines are accomplishing the same purpose, I think. That is, they are getting the tip of the sinking portion of the line down at least as fast as the belly.

JOHN RANDOLPH — Can we move to the subject of sink-tip lines? I think there's confusion about this type of line. I know there are situations in which a sink-tip line is a good fishing instrument, but there are also places where the sink-tip line is a very poor choice. What do you think, Lefty?

LEFTY KREH — I agree, John. First, most people who use a sink-tip line don't really know how to use it correctly. And secondly, they don't understand that a lot of times, a sink-tip line is not doing what they think it is. For example, if you want to get a fly four or five feet down in a stream with a fairly fast current, the average caster — who doesn't know how to make a reach cast or anything — is going to throw his line straight out or slightly downstream. And as soon as the line hits the water, the belly of the line is going to start to pull downstream, lofting the sink-tip line and the fly up and away from the fish. So when I really want to get a fly underwater, most of the time I don't like the sink-tip.

But where I do like sink-tips is for pocket fishing. This is a superb application. What I like about sink-tips in this type fishing is that if I'm casting to bass in a hole surrounded by lily pads, or for trout in a small pocket in a stream, I can quickly drift a streamer or a nymph underwater down through the hole or the pocket and then quickly pick up my line to make another cast. Those are great situations for using a sink-tip line.

Dave Whitlock first told me about an excellent modification for a sink-tip that I have been using ever since. It's fantastic! You take a regular 10-foot sink-tip line and cut off five feet. Is that right, Dave? Five feet?

DAVE WHITLOCK — Yes, four, five, or six feet.

LEFTY KREH — I cut off five feet and put on a popping bug. You'll drive fish crazy. You throw the thing out and you just keep popping — pop, pop, pop — it pops just like a floating line would. But the moment you stop, that little short sinking tip will cause your fly to dive underwater. So you go pop, pop, pop on the surface, then swim, swim, swim underwater, then pop, pop, pop on the surface, and so on. God, it's fabulous what this action does to fish!

DAVE WHITLOCK — The other thing is that little short sink-tip casts a wind-resistant popping bug so well.

LEFTY KREH — I was just going to say that. And you can tuck it back under brush where you can't cast other lines.

DAN BLANTON — Lefty, I'd like to make a point about sink-tips that goes along with what you said because this is really

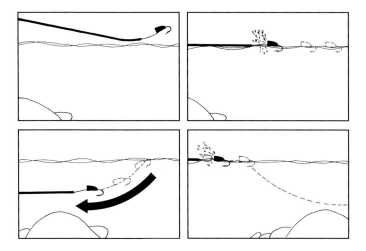

*Popping Bug Presentation with Shortened Sink-Tip Line*

great to me. When I'm lake fishing underwater for trout, my favorite line is not a sink-tip, because if the wind starts to blow, the floating section of the sink-tip line will begin skimming across the water like a sailboat. It'll start to blow across in a big loop, and you immediately lose contact with your fly. Or you get wave action that will plane your fly back up, or cause slack, which means you won't feel subtle hits or even strikes.

DAVE WHITLOCK — I call that stillwater drag!

LEFTY KREH — Well, that's a good way to say it.

DAN BLANTON — So, what I have done in this type situation is to construct what I call an Intermediate sink-tip line. I take an Intermediate line and cut off the last 10 feet or so, and replace it with a splice of a #1 or #2 or #3 sinking line. Since the Intermediate line has neutral buoyancy, it sinks slowly under the water so wind or waves don't bother it, and the minute I start my retrieve, it stops sinking but it doesn't plane back up like a floating line would.

People don't believe me until they see it happen, but I have set hooks in trout as far away as 80 feet with this rig because I have such positive contact and a tight line. So except for pocket fishing such as Lefty just described, I have completely eliminated sink-tip lines from my lake fishing and have gone to the Intermediate sink-tip rig instead.

LEFTY KREH — Me, too!

JIM TEENY — Can I get in one more plug, Lefty? We also have a line called the Mini-tip, which I mentioned before. I designed this line, which has a five-foot sinking tip, for suspended fish and lakeshore fishing . . . you know . . . in water that maybe has some flow, but weeds too. Because just like you guys, I found that the regular 10-foot sink-tip didn't work so well.

I find that even where there are weeds, I can fish a Mini-tip really well in about two to four feet of water, where most of the fish are actively feeding anyway. You look out and see trout or steelhead or salmon, and the reason you can see them is they are not so deep, they are just sitting under there. If you try to use a HI-D line or anything like that, it hits the water with a big splash that spooks them, and they are gone. Or by the time you're ready to retrieve, the line has passed below them. But in a situation where you can take a Mini-tip and a long leader, cast out above the fish and slow drift to them, that's really nice!

*What are the advantages and disadvantages of stretch in the fly line?*

DAVE WHITLOCK — I have something that's really critical as far as my own interest, but I think all of us need to address it. I was wondering if I would get an opportunity to. Lately, I have been testing the Airflo lines and other low-stretch and non-stretch lines for bass fishing and striper fishing. And I have been incredibly intrigued at how you can feel fish and strike fish with those lines. I would like to ask you all what you think about it? Or do you know anything about those lines? Have you used them? Not for trout, necessarily, but if that's what you want to gauge it by . . .

LEFTY KREH — I do not recommend them for casting.

DAVE WHITLOCK — You mean, because they are no-stretch?

LEFTY KREH — Well, that's part of it. But you can't get the coils out of them. They'll just lie on the deck.

DAVE WHITLOCK — Well, the new ones, though, are pretty good about that.

LEFTY KREH — Well, I've tried every line Airflo has ever made, except maybe the last one that they came out with. The other thing about this non-stretch thing, Dave, is that it works against most fishermen. I am not talking about the expert fly fisherman, but about the average guy who sets up on a bonefish and gets all excited, or he sets a little #20 hook on a five-pound brown, and he ain't never caught anything like this! But that's why they use shock gum and stuff in leaders, you know?

DAVE WHITLOCK — Yeah, but I'm talking primarily about largemouth and striped bass.

DAN BLANTON — Can I say something about that in regard to big game — particularly tarpon and sailfish? Now this is what I do and it works for me. I'm not going to say that it works for everybody or that everybody will agree with this, but I'm getting a little older and my reflexes are a little slower than they used to be. So for tarpon fishing, I build stretch into my system. Between my fly line and my Micron backing, I put 100 feet of 30-pound monofilament. I know Flip will probably disagree with this.

LEFTY KREH — Yeah, a lot of the guides in the Keys don't agree with you about this, but I do.

DAN BLANTON — But I even changed my guide's opinion when I was down in Florida after tarpon. Now again, this is not for everybody that's going after tarpon. You see, most people who build stretch into their line don't fight the fish hard enough, which is why they have a problem. I don't. However, I have saved a lot of big rainbows and other big fish that I would have lost otherwise, if I hadn't had some stretch in the line. You see, the stretch compensates for missed bows and line drag. I know some people believe the fly line has enough stretch, all by itself, but I like to put a little bit more into it.

On billfish, I think it is very important. One of the largest sailfish I ever landed was about a 130-pounder. I was with Bill Barnes, and I had the same system built into my billfish line. I hooked this monster sailfish, and it took off in a series of wild jumps and geez, I cleared line, I did everything. And I said to the guide, "Keep close, keep me at about 100 yards. I don't want to be any farther away than that. Back down!" So he put the boat in reverse and the drive shaft fell off! I look at Bill Barnes and Bill looked at me . . . we were astounded! And Bill just calmly looked down, opened the hatch and nonchalantly started looking for bolts and things. He just slapped his head . . . and I had the drag completely backed off this huge reel with about 500 yards of backing peeling away and this big sailfish is headed for South America! It was so far away that it looked like a little ant out there jumping around! And I'm madly

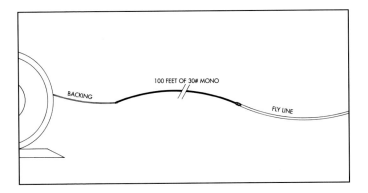

BACKING

100 FEET OF 30# MONO

FLY LINE

cranking all this line. But without that extra stretch, I'm convinced that I would have broken that fish off with my line drag. Now, that's just the way I feel about it!

LEFTY KREH — That's okay! Flip, why don't you like that shock absorber in there?

FLIP PALLOT — Well, if you took a fly line and tied it to a clothes line and got on the other end of it and pulled it, you would amaze yourself at the amount of stretch. Now let's say the fish has made a 100-yard run and now you've added to that another 100 feet of monofilament. The stretch in the backing is another phenomenal thing.

DAN BLANTON — In the Micron backing?

FLIP PALLOT — Well, Micron or Dacron backing, either one. These backing lines stretch like crazy!

LEFTY KREH — Yeah, people say they don't stretch, but they do. They don't stretch as much as monofilament, but . . .

FLIP PALLOT — I know, they don't stretch that much, but 30-pound Micron or Dacron will stretch just as much as your fly line. Now you're adding in there 100 feet of monofilament. What I suggest to you is that once that fish is out there as far as 100 yards, between the stretch in your leader, the stretch in your fly line, and the stretch in your backing, that fish is not stretching your 100 feet of monofilament. You've got so much stretch built into the system already, that what you have done is thrown another connection in there that could get eaten by a little fish or a hound fish or a cuda or something like that . . . you've got two more knots in there . . . lots more potential for a problem — and for nothing, as I see it — because I think the stretch is there anyway. And again, I think that to convince yourself of that, you need to take a whole fly line, tie it to something, take two fingers and pull on it. You'll see it's just like plastic!

DAN BLANTON — Well, the way I convinced myself about this issue is that I fished for a lot of years both ways and I kept track. I think that I saved more fish with the additional stretch the monofilament gave me. But as I said, this is for me, and if you don't believe in it and have your own feelings about it, that's fine! That's what fly fishing is all about!

I will tell you one other advantage of adding this section of monofilament — and this has nothing to do with stretch. You can buy this monofilament in a high visibility fluorescent color. I think the orange works better than the green.

LEFTY KREH — Yes, it does.

DAN BLANTON — . . . And when you have 100 feet of that high vis line out there, it's a super indicator of where you are with your fish and how much line is out; and it's also a real indicator to tracking and fighting your fish. You always know just where it is.

LEFTY KREH — And if the guide ever has to run the boat he can really see it.

DAN BLANTON — It really works great that way, too.

*What about fly line color? Are there places where it is unimportant, or where it is very important?*

LEFTY KREH — I'll let Gary start this because he loves to talk about fly line color!

GARY BORGER — Yeah! Well, I believe the flash off the fly line is important. And that, of course, directly relates to fly line color. I think it's very important in trout fishing, specifically with very spooky fish. There have been many times when I have seen people cast with brightly colored fly lines, and the fish spooks before the line ever gets to the water.

LEFTY KREH — We've talked about that before in reference to New Zealand. It's a classic example.

GARY BORGER — I have taken people to New Zealand. And I have told them, "Do not, under any circumstances, bring fluorescent fly lines." Which results of course, in their bringing only fluorescent fly lines! And so I say, "Okay, if you want to be that way, you fish with a bright line." And I let them fish a day with it and catch zero fish and have the guide just ripping his hair out because he finds a 10-pounder for them that they false cast to with that line, and wham! The fish is gone. They never see it! They never get their final cast to it! And then the guide will have mercy on them and give them an olive-colored or brown-colored fly line. But those are very special circumstances.

However, I translate that backwards by saying that in all fishing situations, I want to always set myself up for the hardiest fish, the spookiest fish. Because you never know when you're blind fishing on the Madison, for example, and you don't see a big fish because of a current line or something. And if you aerialize a bright line over that fish, if it sees it, it's gone! You've lost a chance!

DAVE WHITLOCK — You sometimes never know that!

GARY BORGER — You never know that! So I prefer lines that don't have a lot of flash on the surface of them. Some of the European manufacturers, like Masterline and Airflo, are now producing pastel-colored extruded lines with a somewhat pebbly finish on the surface. It's not real rough, but it's just slightly rough.

LEFTY KREH — It also cuts down reflectiveness.

GARY BORGER — These type lines reduce the reflective flash off the surface of the line, so you can use a line that is relatively brightly colored to your eye, but one that doesn't have a lot of flash while it's moving through the air.

DAN BLANTON — Gary, do you think the fish actually see the color as a bright orange or a bright green, or . . .

GARY BORGER — I don't know if they see that or just see flash off the line.

DAN BLANTON — Reflection!

GARY BORGER — Reflection! And I've seen fish spooked at the reflection off the rod, too. Flash off the fly rod! Now again —this doesn't apply to all fishing situations — but for real spooky fish under clear water conditions, it can be a problem. For example, in the lakes in Mexico where we conduct fly-fishing schools in the summertime, there are browns that cruise along the shoreline, and if you merely raise the rod, they disappear. They see you from 40 feet away! They see that movement, that flash off the rod.

DAN BLANTON — Is it flash or is it movement?

*Dry-fly fishing in the shadow of Lanin Volcano, Malleo River, Argentina.* ➤

DAVE WHITLOCK — The movement!

JIM TEENY — Well, I think the flash off the water helps them to see the movement.

LEFTY KREH — I think it's a combination of the two.

GARY BORGER — Just think in your own mind. You're walking down to a trout stream to your favorite pool, and as you walk across the bridge and look upstream, there, a quarter of a mile away, you see a flash of a fly rod and an orange line going back and forth over the river. Instantaneously, you see that! You may not even see the person who's casting. But you see the flash off that rod and that orange line. And there's a fish 30 feet away that the angler's casting to. You know that the fish sees that. You know it! Whether the fish is concerned or not is another problem. And that's why I say that under circumstances where you are fishing to wild fish, line color and reflection can be a factor.

DAN BLANTON — You mean Del Brown was right all these years painting all of his $300 graphite rods olive drab?

JOHN RANDOLPH — He believes in it! And it makes him a better fly fisherman!

LEFTY KREH — I can't say that I ever lost a fish because of rod flash. But I certainly agree about line color and reflection in many situations. For example, I think Flip would agree that if you cast a bright line in a bright sun over a bonefish, you're going to spook it. But I personally like a real bright line for bonefishing. I also use one for bass fishing, as well as in low-light situations, where the bright color helps indicate to me exactly where the line is, how it's performing, and where the fly is.

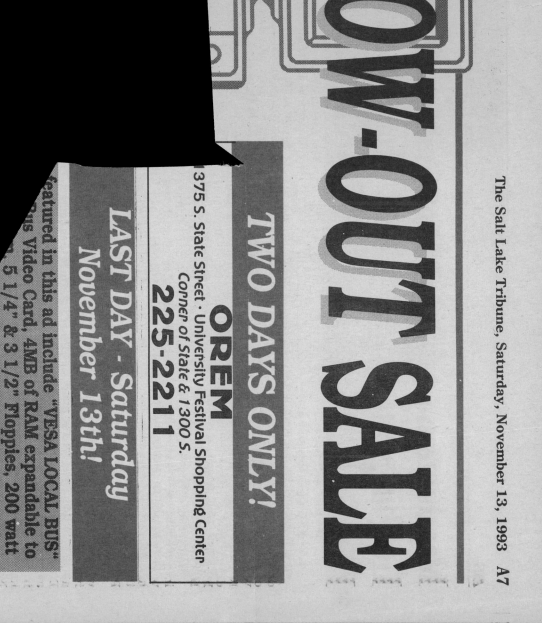

# Mesquite Mayor And His Son Indicted in Sting

THE ASSOCIATED PRESS

LAS VEGAS — Mesquite Mayor Bill Lee and his son were indicted Friday by a Clark County grand jury for allegedly agreeing to accept purported drug money in a Metro Police sting operation.

Lee and his son, Sam, were charged with felony attempted money laundering and burglary and a gross misdemeanor count of conspiracy to launder money.

District Judge Nancy Becker agreed to summon the Lees rather than have them arrested on the charges.

In the sting, a Metro intelligence officer reportedly offered more than $150,000 in tainted money to the mayor for the purchase of his motel in the small city 80 miles northeast of Las Vegas.

Bill and Sam Lee allegedly agreed to accept the money and were caught on videotape talking about how they could launder it through their Burger King restaurant in Mesquite.

Bill Lee, 49, has not commented on the case and has continued to preside as mayor.

The case has become complicated because the undercover detective in the case, Rod Mathis, has pleaded guilty to taking a bribe in an unrelated sting investigation.

But the taint of Mathis' criminal case is not expected to hamper the case against the Lees because of the videotape evidence.

Mathis, according to federal court documents, offered in April to invest hundreds of thousands of dollars of drug money in a business owned by Salt Lake City businessman Jack Turner. Turner was arrested after allegedly accepting a $200,000 check.

But Sandra Andreason, an informant working with Mathis, told Turner that Mathis could make the legal problems "go away" if he paid $50,000, the federal records allege.

Turner's attorney[...] ed the FBI, and a[...] sting operation.[...] over $25,000[...] standing that[...] was due whe[...]

that the charges would be dropped.

Several days later, the records said, Mathis called the prosecutor and told him Turner had been co-operating with law enforcement and was providing information that would lead to other investigations. The court documents said Mathis knew Turner had not provided such helpful information.

On July 28, Turner gave Andreason the second $25,000 — which had been provided by the FBI — and she was arrested.

[...]Mathis, 46, faces a possible 30 [year]s in prison.

DAVE WHITLOCK — Let me ask Gary a question which probably goes right along with that. We are always telling people that when the line is in the air, it scares fish, but once it gets on the water — no matter what color it is — it doesn't seem to scare fish. The principal question that I have about your New Zealand example is that if a person made a low-angle cast with a fluorescent line, and if that line floated by the fish, would it also scare the fish?

GARY BORGER — Yes, it would, in my opinion. In fact, on the west coast of New Zealand, when you fish for the big browns, even in fast water, and you are using an indicator, you cannot use an orange indicator. The fish will spook from the orange indicator!

LEFTY KREH — Well, what about the line that has got the sink tip with the bright orange tip on the fly line?

GARY BORGER — I won't use one!

LEFTY KREH — You know, I'm glad you said that, Gary, because I never used that line because I always felt that was the problem with it!

GARY BORGER — Another thing is that even leader shine is enough to spook these New Zealand fish. Before you begin fishing, all the guides down there take your leader and run it under the felt sole of their boot just to put some mud on it. Just to mud it up a little bit so it's not so shiny.

FLIP PALLOT — You know what I'm hearing here for the first time in my life — something that Gary said triggered this thought. I think I am, and always will be, a believer in very bright lines for saltwater fishing. And I think what the difference is — now finally, it dawns on me — is that in freshwater presentations we're piling the leader up, and the line winds up being a lot closer to the fish than it is in saltwater. In saltwater, we're killing ourselves to straighten the leader out, not to have a single wave in the leader of the fly line. So we can be 12 or 13 feet away from the fish and still use a bright line, and it has no clue that the line is there, especially if we make a nice, low-profile cast and put the leader down correctly in a straight line. But you're basically placing your line a lot closer to your fish in most freshwater fly fishing presentations, even though you may be using a longer leader in some situations.

GARY BORGER — I'll tell you something else that's interesting. Some places — take Silver Creek in Idaho, for example, which gets fished heavily from about the first of June until the end of November. It just gets pounded! And there is one place in there, called Sullivan Spring, which is right under the road. You go up over the hill and you look down, and the water is full of these things that look like tarpon when you first see them. Huge trout! And everybody immediately rushes down there. There are huge trails going down to it! And those fish will not swim under a fly line! They will swim up to it and turn and go away from it.

DAN BLANTON — Flip, do you think that in saltwater one of the reasons why bonefish, for example, are not too concerned about lines in the air, or even on the surface of the water, is that when they are feeding, they are looking down, versus a trout that's looking up?

FLIP PALLOT — Sure, that could have a lot to do with it!

DAN BLANTON — And tarpon are generally looking up. How do you feel about bright lines on tarpon?

FLIP PALLOT — Well, I still use them!

LEFTY KREH — Yeah, I don't see any problem with it.

JOHN RANDOLPH — I'd like to make a point about that fellow at Berkley who did the thing on color.

LEFTY KREH — Yeah, Paul Johnson!

JOHN RANDOLPH — And Gary and I have talked about this. We know that fish see in certain color ranges. But the one thing we know very little about is how they convert perception into action. We do know that rainbows are particularly attracted to flies with the color blue in the pattern. But we don't know an awful lot. And I guess it's because there hasn't been a lot of research done, at least up to this point, on what fish see in the ultraviolet spectrum and how they react to what they see.

LEFTY KREH — But we do know about fluorescence!

JOHN RANDOLPH — Yes, we do! But the corollary is, do we know how fish behave in reacting to what they see.

LEFTY KREH — Yeah, the reaction!

JOHN RANDOLPH — Yes. Once at Los Roques, several of us waded into an area on Parquet flat which was almost like a cul-de-sac. And there were probably 2,000 bonefish in this depression! So it was almost like I had a little bonefishing fly-fishing laboratory! First, I put on a saltwater line that Leon Chandler had given to me for testing. The tip of it had a purple color to it. And I put that right in front of thousands of traveling bonefish — right in front of them — and they would not go past that line. They would go around it. It was almost like someone put a wall out there!

A lot of times on my presentations, because the bonefish were coming directly at the fly at a small angle, all the fish could see was the end of the line, not the entire line or its color. In that situation, as the bonefish swam back and forth over and over again, I could experiment — changing flies, changing lines — just to see how they would react. It was fascinating! But it didn't give me any hard answers. And that's what we're talking about as fly fishermen. We know, for instance, when we go to New Zealand, we observe that when we put a certain kind of color over fish, it terrifies them. So we avoid doing it, but we still don't really have a clue as to why the fish were frightened.

LEFTY KREH — I've encountered the same situation at Christmas Island, John. One time I never moved from one spot on a flat and caught 19 bonefish on 14 different flies!

JOHN RANDOLPH — Now that's a laboratory! Where you control the conditions!

LEFTY KREH — They'd come out, go around, and then come back. And anytime I made a good presentation, I almost always got a strike. Ever since then, I have been convinced that there are certain bonefish flies that will catch more fish than others, but I think bonefish are so opportunistic that they will generally strike if you make a good presentation. I think presentation makes the big difference.

DAN BLANTON — We're mostly alluding to lines on the surface or in the air. But I do know that fish don't like conspicuous fly lines below the surface either.

LEFTY KREH — Absolutely, Dan!

DAN BLANTON — I've seen schools of bonito shy away from white or brightly colored fluorescent lines. But if you throw a dark green or brown or black line into a school, even though they may see it and not like it, the fish don't seem to panic like they do on the bright lines.

LEFTY KREH — I think the Monocore lines, Danny, proved that point completely!

JOHN RANDOLPH — What did they prove?

LEFTY KREH — They proved that the less visible the line the more likely the fish are to be caught.

JOHN RANDOLPH — So then the Monocore line is really like a 100-foot leader.

LEFTY KREH — That's exactly right!

DAN BLANTON — They still see it, but it's not obtrusive to them. I've experimented with it. I have thrown a Monocore line into a wad of happy tarpon and still caught fish. If it was a really flat day, of course, the line slap could scare them. I try never to do that then. I try to just put the leader in the fish, because a 10-foot leader, even when the line's only 10 feet away, doesn't seem to bother them.

OVERLEAF: *A vest for all seasons.*

# CHAPTER FOUR

# HOOKS AND KNOTS

*What is your view on the issue of
using barbless versus barbed hooks?*

FLIP PALLOT — I don't use any barbed hooks and haven't for
a number of years, for anything, even with jigs and plugs.

LEFTY KREH — They are all barbless?

FLIP PALLOT — Yes.

DAVE WHITLOCK — I always tell people that the barb is
something to hold the bait on.

LEFTY KREH — I've used barbless hooks for maybe 25 years!
And I think I catch more fish with barbless hooks.

FLIP PALLOT — You don't catch any less, I don't think.

JIM TEENY — Well, it's easier to set the hook!

LEFTY KREH — Absolutely. I know one writer who says that
a barbless hook gets a deeper penetration and kills fish, but
I can't ever remember killing a fish by using a barbless
hook. I cannot believe that just flicking your hand and taking a barbless hook out is going to damage the fish. And I
cannot believe this business about treble hooks not being
more dangerous. When I was younger I caught a lot of fish
on Mepps spinners, and the way you had to tear their
mouths up to get those hooks out was just awful!

Dave Whitlock — You know, there was a study done on that . . . about these fish and about how much more dangerous a barbless hook is to them than a treble hook! I thought it was such nonsense, so I wrote the guy that did the study and asked him if he would let me put a treble hook and a barbless hook in his mouth, so that we could decide which type hook he would rather have in his own mouth? He didn't answer!

Dan Blanton — I think the answer to this debate depends on the situation. I don't go along with the barbless hook in every case.

Lefty Kreh — Fly fishing for sailfish is the only time I ever use a barbed hook.

Dan Blanton — Well, I disagree even with that, Lefty. I think that using barbless hooks is good technique in certain cases' with trout and the more delicate species . . . or if you're concerned about sticking yourself with a hook.

But let me give you one example where I think you should use a barbed hook, keeping in mind that not everybody fly fishes at the same skill level as the people in this room do. That's on tarpon — I'm not going to fish barbless hooks for tarpon. They are hard enough to land anyway! But what I do is reduce the barb by pinching it down a little bit so that it will penetrate a tarpon's tough mouth better.

And I'll give you another example. When some folks and I were fishing in Alaska last year, there were some ladies in our group that couldn't cast very far. Only on about one cast out of 30 were they able to reach the water where some silvers were holding. Finally, when they did hook a fish, they would then foul up one way or the other — by trying to clear their line or get it on the reel, they'd slack off pressure, or what have you. So they were losing almost all their fish. These fish were just coming unbuttoned! Now I've lost many salmon with barbless hooks. Again, they just come unbuttoned. Steelhead come unbuttoned for a variety of reasons, too. And I'm supposed to know what I'm doing!

Anyway, to see if I could help out in this situation, I went over to one of the women who was really getting pretty frustrated and handed her one of my barbed flies. We tied it on and she started landing a few fish. But then the guide came over and began chewing her out for fishing with a barbed hook. I took this guy aside and told him I thought he was getting carried away with his conservation ethic, because every one of those silvers was going to die anyway. They were not Atlantic salmon. Furthermore, I told him, "With all the teeth in their heads, what do you think these big bucks are going to be doing to each other in a matter of a few days? They are going to be biting big chunks out of each other as they fight for the reds."

With a small barb, I can generally get the hook out pretty easily, and if the fish is gill hooked, I'll cut the leader.

I really believe, again, that we have a lot of situations where barbs aren't going to hurt the fish. Just last Wednesday, I talked to my guide on the Madison about this. He said he didn't smash down barbs in hooks, because if he did, half of his clients wouldn't land fish!

Let's face it, inexperienced people will not always land fish. And I think there are certain fish that a barbed hook doesn't hurt at all. I have caught plenty of striped bass on a barbed hook that came out easily enough. So I really believe that in certain circumstances, there is nothing wrong with the barbed hook and others where you need to use some good judgment.

LEFTY KREH — Gary, do you have any preference?

GARY BORGER — There are times when I prefer not to use barbless hooks. One of those times is when I'm fishing for trout with relatively small flies in weedy situations. Because what happens is that weeds hang on the leader, then slide down and act just like a hook disgorger, causing the fly to pop right out. The weight of the material in the fly pattern sliding down back against the hook will actually force the fly out of the fish's mouth.

Now if you are not worried about landing the fish — and most of the time when I'm fly fishing I don't give a dang whether I land a fish or not! Under those circumstances, I just pinch the barb down and go for it and if it gets disgorged by the weeds, well, so what, who cares? Just go catch another one!

But barbless hooks will come out easier than barbed hooks. That's why we fish with a barbless hook. Because when it comes time to take the hook out, you just go flick, and it comes out!

But when a big trout jumps with a big barbless streamer in its mouth and shakes its head, it can throw the hook right out. I have seen them do it lots and lots of times. So in fishing for those big ones, I pinch the barb just almost shut so that the little remainder of barb can catch a tiny bit of flesh and keep the hook from flying out.

I certainly don't think it's necessary to have a big barb on a hook. I like micro barbs. In fact I would like for them to make barbs even smaller than they do now on the Tiemco and Dai-Riki hooks. Very, very tiny barbs, just to give the hook the tiniest bit of purchase so it will stay in there under those very specific kinds of circumstances.

LEFTY KREH — Flip, you have caught hundreds of tarpon, which probably is the biggest jumper and most acrobatic of all fish. Do you feel barbless hooks come out with tarpon?

FLIP PALLOT — I can't tell any difference. Tarpon are so darn hard to hook anyway. I almost feel that you might get a little better purchase without the barb to begin with. I'll tell you the crazy thing that I have seen. I don't know if any of you have had this experience, but I have hooked tarpon with and without barbs on a fly. And I have hooked them right by the boat and I have seen them jump right by the boat the very first time and they will have the hook in one place in their mouth, and then three jumps later, they have the hook in another place, and later, it's in another place altogether. I've had hooks just walk all around on tarpon. And on snook, as well. Snook will do the same thing. I know it sounds crazy, but it happens!

LEFTY KREH — I spent four years back in the late 50s and early 60s fishing one rod for smallmouth bass — this was mostly plug tackle, but I used popping bugs and streamers too. For an hour or so, I would fish a plug barbless, and then I would use one with barbed hooks. And after four years — and I kept pretty good records — I realized that I had caught more fish on barbless hooks than I had on the barbed. And I can't see where jumping fish get off any easier with barbless hooks. The only thing I seem to have a problem with is sailfish.

DAVE WHITLOCK — One thing to consider is that certainly a barbless hook will last four or five times longer than a barbed hook, because most of the damage done to a fly is not done by the fish, but by the fisherman trying to remove it from the fish's mouth. So a lot of people complain that these little flies don't hold up. So just from a pure economical standpoint, people need to know that.

LEFTY KREH — I hadn't thought of that. That's a good point.

DAVE WHITLOCK — Another thing is, there's no difference, so far as the fish is concerned, between stainless steel and bronze hooks, even though a lot of people think so. The enzyme action on a stainless steel hook is exactly the same as it is on a bronze hook. That hook is going to fall out sooner or later, whether the hook is stainless steel or bronze, because bacteria gets in there, and that's what causes the hook to fall out. But most people think that a stainless steel hook will stay in a fish indefinitely. And that's just not true! And I wish you guys would start telling them so.

DAN BLANTON — I do, Dave. I have lost literally hundreds and hundreds of striped bass in the dock pilings around San Francisco Bay because I couldn't turn them and they finally broke off. In all the years that I have fished out there, having that happen — and you know, the salinity factor in the bay is much higher than in the open ocean because it's shallow and there's the effect of evaporation and all that — I have never, never seen a striped bass floating around dead with a fly stuck in its mouth.

DAVE WHITLOCK — No, it doesn't happen. But so many people will say that it does.

LEFTY KREH — Well, I can see why some people don't fish with stainless steel hooks because carbon steel hooks are stronger and hold a better point, but that's a different issue.

DAVE WHITLOCK — But their point is, though, that they think the fish is going to swim around suffering . . .

LEFTY KREH — I had a biologist tell me that a fish develops a sore wherever the hook is located, and eventually, regardless of what kind of hook it is, the fish will expel the hook from its mouth.

*What are the most important considerations about building a good knot?*

FLIP PALLOT — Closing the knot completely, to me, is *the* most important consideration.

JOHN RANDOLPH — Why is that? What if you don't?

FLIP PALLOT — Then it slips and fails. And I guess the only other considerations that I can think of in building a good knot are starting with good materials and trimming the knot properly when you have built it. Because sometimes trimming knots incorrectly can cause problems — not necessarily a knot failure but other fishing problems.

JIM TEENY — Well, I think one of the most important things . . . maybe I'm not going to cover it right, but when you take two monofilaments and put them together, they are almost always different pound-test strengths. So, it's critical to get them to marry properly so that when you draw them up you don't have an abrasion or a weak spot. For example, you should not try to marry 40-pound monofilament to 10-pound monofilament. There's a certain point where the big line will overpower the small one.

DAN BLANTON — When I was with Berkley, we did a lot of knot testing, trying to come up with consistently good knots. So, based on this experience, I think you need to choose knots that are consistent. Lubricating the knot is also an important factor. Another thing also — a lot of people don't realize this — is that when you draw the knot down, you have to start and stop without any hesitation. When you start to draw the knot down, even if you lubricate it with saliva, the friction of the two pieces of monofilament working against each other is going to generate heat. And if you stop for any reason, the monofilament is going to bind and you're not going to get a good, clean knot.

LEFTY KREH — That's one of the major reasons why blood knots fail on people.

DAN BLANTON — And you shouldn't jerk a knot together — you don't just grab it and yank on each end in opposite directions. But on the other hand, you shouldn't draw the knot up too slowly either. Because if you do it too slowly, the same thing occurs. It's the same effect as having made a pause. So there's an in-between point where you just simply pull the pieces together firmly and relatively quickly. I've already said that lubricating the knot is important, but I have also found that some monofilaments don't do well if you wet them. Some of them already have some lubricant built into the material, such as Maxima Green, for example. If you lubricate that type monofilament — not so much on small hooks, but certainly on the larger hooks — you can't even tie a knot. It simply will not draw down. It must be dry to draw down well. So you have to find that out for yourself by just experimenting with the various monofilaments that are on the market.

LEFTY KREH — And, of course, you guys know that we did a knot book and I probably know 200 knots. And there is no question in my mind that the two most important things about knots are, first, that any knot, whether you tie it with a 2-inch hose or 8X-monofilament, will break when it begins to slip. That's the most important thing in any knot. You can take a knot that is really not mechanically a very good knot. But if you tie it real tight, really close it, and compare it to another knot which by design engineering is a better knot, but which you didn't tie down tight, it will fail quicker than the first knot.

That's why when people write about knots and tell you that with a certain diameter of line you need to make so many turns, they are reporting what they have found out by machine testing. So that if you have less turns than that, then you don't have enough turns to keep the knot from slipping. Or if you put too many turns on the knot, you've got so many that you simply can't draw the knot tight enough to keep it from slipping.

The second important thing about knots, which I have never seen in writing anywhere until Mark Sosin and I published our latest knot book, is that it's extremely difficult — it's not impossible, but very difficult — to join two pieces of monofilament which do not have the same basic flexibility. If you take a real stiff piece of monofilament and try to tie it to a real limp piece, you'll find it's extremely difficult to do. So when you can, it pays to use monofilament that has the same apparent limpness. This is something I find that a lot of people who make their own tapered leaders don't recognize. They just pick out a couple pieces of monofilament and start tying, and they have a lot of problems.

Another thing that's important to keep in mind when tying the blood knot, which is one of the most popular fly-fishing knots, is that after a lot of people have constructed the basic pattern, as they are starting their pull to tighten the knot, they pause. And what happens as a result, as Dan mentioned, is that they've built up an awful lot of heat in the monofilament.

And when they pause, the knot instantly takes a set. You've probably all seen this effect yourselves. After you've made a poor tie on a blood knot, if you will take the strands apart, you'll notice the heavier line has the appearance of a coiled spring, probably because you paused.

And I don't want put a bad rap on anybody, so I won't give the manufacturer's name here, but there is one brand of monofilament with which you absolutely cannot tie a good surgeon's knot. So everybody should keep in mind that there are some types of monofilament that simply do not produce good knots.

GARY BORGER — I think everybody agrees that lubricating the knot is extremely important. And then, like Flip said, getting it closed. When I pull knots tight — with a certain speed like Dan has described, you know, not too slow, but not too fast — after I have closed the knot, I stretch the monofilament and hold it in a stretched position for a few seconds so that it can stretch out in the knot and get as tight as it can possibly get. It's like tying a knot in a rubber band. When you stretch a rubber band the material gets smaller. But if you will hold the knot in the stretched position for a few seconds, the monofilament will stretch in the knot and that will help make it very, very tight. So I always stretch the mono.

LEFTY KREH — Wouldn't you agree, also, Gary, that after you have tied monofilament to your hook, you should always test the strength of the knot then, not later on a fish?

GARY BORGER — Absolutely. Another point that I'd like to make about the blood knot. I know a lot of people use the surgeon's knot to tie tippets. But I prefer the blood knot. I grew up tying only the blood knot, so I'm more comfortable with it. And I like the blood knot because it's small in diameter and makes a neater appearance on the line.

But there's one more thing. I also discovered something about tying blood knots when I started playing around with leaders — connecting relatively large diameters to smaller diameters. For example, I began stepping down from say, 20-pound monofilament to 12-pound monofilament in one shot. I didn't progress down from 20-pound to 18, 16, 14, 12, 10-pound, and so on. I just went from 20-pound right down to 14-pound, and then from 14-pound right down to

10-pound. But when I began connecting these pieces with the blood knot, I realized that if I took more turns with the lighter diameter monofilament, I would get a knot that was balanced by making fewer turns of the heavier diameter monofilament to which I was connecting it. So now, for example, I will take four turns with the heavy stuff and six turns with the light. Or five turns with the heavy and seven with the light. But I never go more than five or seven turns.

LEFTY KREH — You might want to try this, Gary. Flip has a knot that is the best blood knot I have ever seen. Most of the time wouldn't you say it has 100-percent strength, Flip? What you do with this method is to actually double the end of the light line and make it . . .

GARY BORGER — Yeah, that's the way Stu Apte does!

LEFTY KREH — Well, that's the basic Stu Apte type blood knot. That's a good point, though, Gary. Whenever you make blood knots with monofilament of widely dissimilar diameters, if you make more turns on the lighter material than the heavier, you'll get a better knot.

JOHN RANDOLPH — I was just going to say that as the diameter of the monofilament in my leaders gets larger, I need fewer wraps because of the inherent increase in friction because of the larger diameter and surface area. And then as I get down to lighter and lighter tippet material, I need more wraps to accomplish the same thing.

And the other point is that you have to take more care with the small tippet knots, because they are the weakest point in your leader system.

DAN BLANTON — No matter which type of knot you choose, one other thing to consider when you're fishing with heavily weighted or large saltwater flies, and you are not using a shock tippet or heavy mono or wire — just using your regular tippet, or your class tippet — is that you should take two turns of the tippet material through the eye of the hook. Because some of the heavier hooks will wear through the monofilament. Even as you're casting they will hinge and cause wear. And when you're fighting the fish the monofilament will move from left to right, or up and down, or back and forth, depending upon how you apply the angles. Before I started making double turns through the eye of the hook, I would often lose fish after putting a lot of angles on them. I literally wore a single strand out. Going through twice this way does two things. It gives you two strands to wear on, and the two strands will actually help trap the tag end and keep it from slipping.

DAVE WHITLOCK — One of the things that relates to what Dan said is, no matter how good a knot you have, you will get wear on the hook. So after you have fished with a knot for a little while, you should change it.

Also, I want to get into the effect of moisture on knots, that is, how much strength they lose when they get wet.

LEFTY KREH — We've conducted experiments on that! If you average it out, the average monofilament loses 12 percent of its line strength, which includes the knot, after it has been soaked in water for more than an hour. But you can waterproof knots with a sealant and keep them stronger.

DAVE WHITLOCK — Well, I will tell you what I am doing regularly now. As I am tightening my knot, I coat it with Zap-A-Gap. I call that using chemicals to strengthen the knot rather than just your own physical strength.

LEFTY KREH — If you could totally waterproof the knot, you should save that lost 12 percent of the line strength, which is a lot on a light leader.

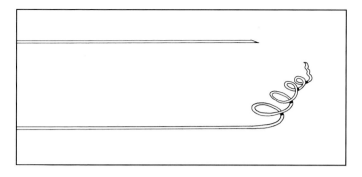

*Sure Indicator of a Poor Knot*

DAN BLANTON — You know, when you think about it, there are so many things in fly fishing that you, as an angler, cannot control. But you can control your knots! There is no reason to lose a fish to a bad knot. I think on most knot failures, the angler, if he really thinks about it, knows that he had tied a bad knot. I know every time I've tied a bad knot, it's because I've gotten lazy and complacent and haven't cut it off and retied it. And invariably, that's when I'm going to get a hook-up on a big fish and lose it! So, my advice is, if the knot doesn't feel right when you draw it down, or it doesn't look right, cut it off and start again.

LEFTY KREH — Yeah, and another thing we all know — but we assume that a lot of people who are going to read these books won't know — is that if you lose a fish and the end of your tippet looks like a curly pigtail, you know you did not close your knot properly. That's a sure indicator! No one can lie his way out of that!

DAVE WHITLOCK — If we are really concerned about knot strength and leader strength, shouldn't we always make sure that the material we are using is up to strength?

LEFTY KREH — Most monofilaments being manufactured today are actually stronger than it says on the spool.

DAN BLANTON — But in that same vein, Dave, there are things you can do to protect your monofilament. First of all, you don't put monofilament out in the sun in high temperatures and expose it to ultraviolet light. That's one of the worst things you can do to monofilament!

LEFTY KREH — And you don't carry leaders with sharp objects in your pockets. One of the things that most people don't realize about monofilament is that it is a lot like a garbage bag. If Dave and I were to pull a garbage bag real tight, and Gary took a razor blade and sliced a linear strip off the garbage bag, we wouldn't be able to pull the garbage bag apart. But if Dave and I pulled the garbage tight and Gary nicked the bag with the razor blade, the whole bag would just shear right in half! Well, monofilament is just like that. Whenever you nick it, you drastically reduce its strength. That's why it's a good idea when you catch a fish of any size to clip off some tippet and replace it, particularly with the small-diameter tippets we use on trout.

*What are the essential knots that an angler needs to know to be a competent freshwater fly fisherman?*

DAVE WHITLOCK — Well, I get by with approximately three knots. But my favorite knot for connecting all my tackle together is a Duncan loop.

LEFTY KREH — Or some people call it a Uni-knot.

DAVE WHITLOCK — Yes, a Uni-knot. I use it to tie backing to my fly line, fly line to the leader, and tippets to the leader.

So I guess I would always go with that, as well as the double surgeon's knot. And then some type of knot to tie on a shock tippet. And those knots would be the three I'd use.

JOHN RANDOLPH — I would agree with that.

GARY BORGER — I use a surgeon's loop to connect the backing onto the reel. I use the Uni-knot to attach the backing to the fly line, and then I put a 12 to 15-inch long connector of 20-pound monofilament on the other end of the line so I can change leaders by looping them on and off quickly.

I use the Uni-knot to attach this connector, but I modify it into a needle knot. I stick a needle into the end of the fly line about 1/8-inch, and then poke it out the side. I remove the needle and thread a piece of the 20-pound connector through the hole made by the needle, and then tie the mono onto the fly line with a Uni-knot. It should be seated just above the point where the monofilament comes out of the side of the line. This way, I've got the connector coming right out of the center of the fly line. Then I tie a perfection loop on the other end of the connector.

I also use a perfection loop on the butt of the leader — so that I can made a rapid connector attachment — and then use a blood or surgeon's knot to build the leader and attach my tippets.

LEFTY KREH — What knot do you use for the fly?

GARY BORGER — The fly? Normally, I just use a straight old clinch knot.

LEFTY KREH — Improved clinch?

GARY BORGER — No, straight old clinch! The biggest problem I have found with people tying the clinch knot is they always pull the short end. When they pull the short end, the loops can't spin back on themselves, and they don't get a knot. Then they make about two casts, and the fly comes off or the fish comes off. But if you hold the short end, pull the clinch knot tight, and hold it until it's all stretched out, you'll produce a very strong knot. I never have had any problems with a clinch knot.

DAVE WHITLOCK — Do you agree with that?

LEFTY KREH — No, I don't agree with that at all!

DAVE WHITLOCK — Okay, well, he's the first person that I have ever heard say that and I'm surprised.

GARY BORGER — Well, I've caught thousands and thousands of trout, and I have never had a problem.

LEFTY KREH — That's because you're a good fisherman. But I tell you, if you take two hooks and tie your clinch knot on one and tie an improved clinch on the other and take two pair of pliers, grip one hook with one pair of pliers and grip the other hook with the other pair of pliers, then first slow-draw them and then make a few jerks. I think you would find that your plain clinch knot is not anywhere near the strength of an improved clinch. It will break every time before the improved clinch knot does.

GARY BORGER — Well, Lefty, I just don't break fish off with the clinch knot.

LEFTY KREH — Well, I think that's your fishing ability and not your knot!

DAN BLANTON — In freshwater fishing I loop a lot of my leader butts like Gary. I like the loop. In fact, most of my lines have loops. But also I think a good nail knot or speedy nail knot is important. I connect all my butt sections together with a surgeon's knot. And I don't use a double surgeon's, I use a triple surgeon's knot. I think going through three times is much stronger than going through twice.

With the exception of very small dry flies, my fly to tippet connection is always what they now call a Trilene knot. It's interesting. I have known this knot since I was a kid. My Dad showed it to me. We used to call it the fisherman's knot. You go through the eye ring twice, come around five turns, and it's not improved.

LEFTY KREH — You don't want to improve it.

DAN BLANTON — You don't want it improved! When I was at Berkley, one of the big considerations there, of course, was knots. They tested hundreds of them. And it reminds me of something Lefty used to say, "Knot testing machines don't have an opinion." And did we test knots! We would get 20 women who worked down in the assembly plant and ask them to tie about 100 knots each, and then we would test those on the R2D2 knot-testing machine.

To avoid the problem of the monofilament wearing on the hook that I talked about earlier, Berkley wanted to develop a knot that would have two strands going through the eye. So I showed them the old fisherman's knot. And I really had to convince them to try it! But once they did, they proved to themselves that it would work. That's what they now call a Trilene knot. And that's the one that I use all the time, except if I'm putting on shock tippet, or if I want a free-swinging fly. For that, I use the Uni-knot.

LEFTY KREH — That Trilene knot you're talking about, Dan. That knot is named that way because when Mark Sosin and I wrote our first knot book, Berkley paid us $500 to rename it "Trilene." And Mark and I told them, "Hey, we've got forty other knots in this book, and we'd be happy to rename them for $500 each too!"

JIM TEENY — I am not that great of a knot tyer, okay, but I do use the nail knot. I tie the nail knot without a nail to my fly line, and then I do a blood knot. Or sometimes I use the triple surgeon's. And then I just put a clinch knot for the fly. And I do not improve it when I'm using the heavier pound-test monofilaments.

LEFTY KREH — Because you want it to break, huh?

JIM TEENY — No, it's just because I don't have any problems. If I had problems, I would improve it. I do improve on the lighter pound-test monofilament, because it has more of a tendency to slip, I think. But with the heavier weight mono-filaments, like 12-pound and 15-pound, they seem to snug up nice for me with an unimproved clinch. But I do leave a little bit of tag. I don't clip it close.

LEFTY KREH — So if it slips, it's still going to tighten itself.

JIM TEENY — Exactly! I don't cut it right to the end. So, basi-cally, that's what I do. And so far, I'm surviving.

FLIP PALLOT — I think there are only about four or five knots that I use in freshwater. I use a Bimini Twist to form the loop in the back end, just because I tie Bimini Twists so much that I just don't even think about anything else. I use a nail knot to attach backing to the fly line. I use blood knots for the leader, and I use an improved clinch knot or a Uni-knot to attach the fly.

LEFTY KREH — I like loops. You can use a surgeon's loop, which I do when I'm in a hurry sometimes on the water. But when I have the time, I really prefer to tie a Bimini Twist in my backing and then whip a loop with a bobbin in my fly line. Then I put a loop on the front end. For that I used to use a surgeon's loop. But Sosin and I found a new loop knot which I now prefer for my front loops. I've been writing about it in all my books lately, but I think it bears repeating here because it's just so good I don't want any-body to miss out on it! It's a 100-percent strength knot, even with 8X-leader material. It is every bit as quick to tie as a clinch knot or an improved clinch, or anything like that. And I feel it is vastly superior to the Uni-knot. I use it now for all my streamers, nymphs, and popping bugs. You can make it for little flies — I use it on all flies that I want to swing freely on the hook — or you can use it for making loops in monofilament. And it's really a pretty simple knot. We call it a non-slip mono loop.

And, finally for my dry-fly work, I really like George Harvey's dry-fly knot.

DAN BLANTON — Since we're talking about attaching backing, I would like to mention one technique that I have been using for attaching backing on fly lines for big game fish, particularly when I'm using a Monocore line. I think I wrote a piece about this in *Fly Fisherman*. You see, we were having problems with the Monocore line and were trying to figure out a way to keep from stripping the finish off. Well, the solution is to use heavy braided monofilament leader butt material.

LEFTY KREH — You get the 30-pound?

DAN BLANTON — I get the big stuff, yes, the heaviest I can get of the braided monofilament leader butt material. I slide the braided monofilament over the backing maybe four, five, or six inches, serve it down — and for our readers that aren't familiar with that fly-tying term, that's taking thread and making a series of circular wraps on top of the very end of the braided  monofilament that you had slid up on the backing line to prevent it from fraying — or you can tie a nail knot to hold the monofilament down tight against the backing line, and clip it close to finish off the connection neatly. Then I simply tie a Bimini Twist into the other end of the braided loop stuff. Or you could tie a surgeon's loop.

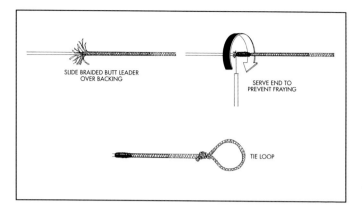

SLIDE BRAIDED BUTT LEADER OVER BACKING

SERVE END TO PREVENT FRAYING

TIE LOOP

*Making a Backing Connection with Braided Monofilament Leader Butt Material*

That braided connection will not pull off nor will it break! You'll break your fly line first! I use that method with all my fly lines and shooting heads now.

LEFTY KREH — It's real quick and easy! You know what he's saying, Dave?

DAVE WHITLOCK — I think I do. You better tell me some more. You mean that sleeve stuff?

LEFTY KREH — It's called braided leader material. It comes with 50 yards on a spool, as I recall, and you want to get the 30-pound. I don't think you can get it any bigger than that. You take this braided monofilament, and you slide it up on the backing a few inches, like Dan was explaining. It will start to fray, and when it does, you fold it back on itself, then shove it on up, and serve it down. It only takes literally two or three minutes to set it up.

DAVE WHITLOCK — You don't put any kind of cement or anything on it?

LEFTY KREH — You only serve just enough to cover about an 1/8-inch of the braided monofilament at the end, so you'll maintain the maximum amount of flexibility in the connection, and then you can put a little Pliobond or Goop on it. The unglued portion surrounding the line acts like a Chinese finger and doesn't slip.

DAN BLANTON — I also do the same thing to splice two or three different densities of line together. I take a sleeve of this stuff and slide it up on both pieces of line. Then I run my fly lines together until they butt up against each other and serve over the braided monofilament in that area. And I've got an instant splice. I've spliced many broken fly lines together this way.

DAVE WHITLOCK — Where do you get that stuff?

DAN BLANTON — Well, I know Cortland sells it, for one.

*What are the additional essential knots that an angler needs to know to be a competent saltwater fly fisherman?*

FLIP PALLOT — Well, we've already discussed it, but you must have — *absolutely must have* — the Bimini Twist. You're just not a competent saltwater fly fisherman without it! Then, in addition to the knots we've discussed, I think you must have the Albright knot — maybe the Huffnagle knot or the Albright knot. I prefer the Albright knot because it can be trimmed up much closer, and you don't have tag ends catching seaweed and things like that.

LEFTY KREH — And you can use the Albright knot to connect wire to monofilament, which you can't do with the Huffnagle knot.

FLIP PALLOT — And also, the Albright knot is a good knot for attaching heavy shock tippets to lighter class tippets.

LEFTY KREH — I think the unfortunate thing about the Albright knot is that while it's a very good knot that has served fly-fishing purposes well for about thirty years, because it's an old knot, people think it is not as good as some of the new knots. My own feeling is that it's better than some of the newer knots.

JIM TEENY — The only thing I know is that I use the Albright knot for joining the backing to the fly line, and it's my favorite.

LEFTY KREH — It works real well in a lot of situations.

DAN BLANTON — I agree with Flip on the Bimini Twist. In fact, I understand there are a lot of people today who are suggesting that the Spider Hitch is the better knot, or as good a knot, and I just can't go along with that. The Bimini Twist is the only knot that I know of that enables you to form loops in your line and maintain 100-percent strength.

But I happen to like the Huffnagle knot or the uptight knot better than the Albright knot. One of the reasons is simply that by the time I tie up a 50 or 100 leaders using the Albright knot, my fingers and thumbs are so sore trying to work that knot together that I am in a lot of pain. Also, I think that if you don't tie the Albright knot correctly, it can fail on you.

I like a loop knot on my shock tippet, but I think some anglers — I'm not sure how Flip feels about it — like to come straight to the fly with a snell. Some even like a three-turn clinch knot.

My favorite loop knot is still the Homer Rhode knot. I rarely have any problems with it.

Finally, when I'm building a leader for heavy saltwater work, say, joining a 50 or 60-pound butt section to a 25 or 30-pound shock tippet and then joining that to my class tippet, I find that in joining the heavy butt section to the shock tippet, blood knots really don't work well, and surgeon's knots end up being too big. So, what I end up using are Uni-knots back to back. Those work well for me.

LEFTY KREH — Flip, how do you feel about tying the tarpon fly with heavy shock leader material? Do you like the loop knot or do you like a straight tie?

FLIP PALLOT — I come down hard for a straight tie with an unimproved clinch knot.

LEFTY KREH — Three-turn clinch knot?

FLIP PALLOT — It's a two-and-a-half turn, unimproved.

LEFTY KREH — What do you think of snelling?

FLIP PALLOT — You know, I think snelling is probably fine.

LEFTY KREH — It takes three times as long to tie.

FLIP PALLOT — Yes, it takes a longer time to tie, and I think that if I were going to snell, because I use floating lines more, I'd probably have to turn the ring of the eye down or something. So I just use the clinch knot.

DAN BLANTON — I am a still trying to be the most efficient fisherman I can be, so I do a lot of experimenting, even though I haven't been fishing with flies as long as some of you guys have. I have discovered that I have a real problem with snelling, because even though I pre-stretch my 100-pound monofilament, it's not always 100-percent stretched. Moreover, a lot of times, if you fix that line hard against the eye of the hook as you complete your snell, your fly may have a tendency to turn, or your hook may not be quite in plane, and then you get a little curve in the monofilament. The result being that the fly will roll and twist, and you won't get a good retrieve.

But with a loop knot, the fly is always going to find its balance and swing. I mean, you can even have a little twist in your line and that loop will still let your fly work properly. You will foul the line sometimes, but you can foul any line. The benefits of snelling are not worth the effort.

FLIP PALLOT — I've never done it.

LEFTY KREH — I tried it for awhile, but I went back to plain old loops. Also, the one thing that most inexperienced anglers don't understand about why we use the Bimini Twist is that knots are generally weaker than the lines you're connecting. But the Bimini Twist is one of the very few knots that always has 100-percent strength. So when you take two pieces of 12-pound monofilament and make a Bimini Twist, you're ending up with two pieces of 12-pound, which equals 24-pound test. But many people don't understand that.

DAN BLANTON — There's another factor to that, too, Lefty. All monofilaments have what they call stress-fatigue resistance. It's the ability to elongate or stretch and return. And a Bimini Twist, because of the nature of the knot — because of its over-wrapping — when you pull a Bimini Twist it will sort of uncoil, as if it were releasing tension. It stretches and comes back to its original shape without slipping. In other words, it's like a spring. People say, and I've read this so many times, that the Bimini Twist is this awful, complicated knot. It isn't. Learning to tie my shoes when I was a kid was more complicated than tying a Bimini twist.

LEFTY KREH — If you practice, you can tie a Bimini Twist in 10 or 12 seconds.

# THE SYMPOSIUM PARTICIPANTS' SELECTION OF ESSENTIAL FLY-FISHING KNOTS

### The Freshwater Knots

Clinch Knot (unimproved, improved,
and three-turn)
Blood Knot (conventional, simple,
and Stu Apte Improved)
Surgeon's Knot (double and triple)
Uni-Knot (Duncan Loop)
Trilene Knot
Surgeon's Loop (double and triple)
Perfection Loop
Non-slip Mono Loop
Speedy Nail Knot
George Harvey Dry-Fly Knot

### Additional Knots for Saltwater

Bimini Twist
Albright Knot
Huffnagle Knot
Homer Rhode Loop Knot

Note: Illustrations of these knots appear in the Appendix. Or for more detailed instructions, see *Practical Fishing Knots II*, by Mark Sosin and Lefty Kreh (Lyons & Burford, Publishers, 31 West 21 Street, New York, New York 10010, 1991).

OVERLEAF: *Atlantic salmon flies and tackle, Gaula River, Norway.*

CHAPTER FIVE

# FLIES

*For the beginning fly fisherman, what would you recommend as an initial fly selection: for trout? for bonefish? for various other species of saltwater fish?*

LEFTY KREH — Gary, let's start with trout. What are your recommendations?

GARY BORGER — One of the problems of giving a selection of flies for trout is that trout eat so many different things that they can get selective to a lot of stuff.

For opportunistic times, or for underwater flies, just take something that has a lot of motion to it. Go get Teeny Nymphs, soft-hackle flies, leech patterns, Zonkers, Marabou streamers — any flies that have a lot of motion so that the trout is attracted to them. The fish sees the fly, it looks like something alive, and it comes and takes it.

For dry-fly fishing during opportunistic times, I like flies that look generally like food items. I mean, you could fish in a meadow stream with any of the terrestrial patterns. In bigger waters, you could fish things like a Royal Wulff or a Humpy or an Adams — you know, the standard kind of flies that we think of.

But during a hatch, it's a totally different story. During a hatch when trout are feeding selectively, you've got to match the hatch. So rather than trying to list every kind of food organism that there is, and every kind of pattern that there is to match it, you just have to keep this in mind: the selective feeding times are when you are going to catch the most fish the quickest, if you have the right fly and you drive it right. The fly and the driver. That's the game!

DAVE WHITLOCK — But wouldn't it be good advice, though — because you travel a lot as all of us to — to point out that there are different hatches in different areas, and that you need to find out locally what's going on? Because, I mean, what may work in one area won't work in another.

GARY BORGER — Always go and ask! And your guide ought to know. If he doesn't, get a new guide!

LEFTY KREH — What are your recommendations, Dave?

DAVE WHITLOCK — Well, on the trout fly selections, I think if you just took four flies or six flies, you know, just to get someone into catching trout. If they are pretty inexperienced about hatches and all that, you should certainly get someone started with a dry surface attractor — such as an Adams or a Royal Wulff — along with a couple of flies that look like bugs that are relatively visible to trout, as well as to the angler, in the relatively popular sizes — #12 to #16 — something not real big but not real small either. Add to that a soft-hackle wet fly, one or two nymph patterns, and then a Marabou streamer and maybe something like a Zonker. This would probably cover the gamut of opportunistic patterns — something floating on the top, something swimming or drowning just under the surface of the water, and something swimming or drifting deep down.

LEFTY KREH — Dave, one of the things that we ought to bring out is that there are really two kinds of dry-fly fishing for trout in the United States. In the West, it's predominantly dry-fly fishing for wild trout. In the East — particularly throughout most of the Northeast these days — much of the dry-fly fishing is fishing to hatchery trout that don't hone in on hatches. Hatchery fish will eat anything that looks good and drifts naturally towards them.

So I want to emphasize that the fly fisherman in the Northeast who is fishing almost exclusively to hatchery fish that have only been in the water system a few weeks, or even just a few days, could possibly fall into the error of misinterpreting a lot of what we have to say here about fly selection on natural trout waters. And as a result, he might conclude that this pattern selection process, which can be critical and pretty complicated sometimes when you're dealing exclusively with wild fish, really doesn't apply to hatchery water. The approach you have suggested, Dave, is just right, I think, for hatchery water.

Flip, why don't you tackle the bonefish and saltwater fly recommendations — perhaps a small general selection of saltwater flies, half a dozen, maybe.

FLIP PALLOT — Okay! Specifically for bonefish, probably the single most effective fly is the Clouser Deep Minnow. But I'm ashamed to say that when Lefty first showed me one . . .

LEFTY KREH — I love to hear him tell this!

FLIP PALLOT — . . . I wanted to have him committed!

LEFTY KREH — Flip carried it around in his box for awhile and wouldn't even use it . . . until nothing else worked!

FLIP PALLOT — It's the stupidest looking thing!

LEFTY KREH — Now he has a box with nothing else in it! That chartreuse and white — white with a chartreuse back — and the white with the tan back, are the only two Clousers you need for bonefish.

FLIP PALLOT — It's the single best bonefish fly there is.

LEFTY KREH — I've never seen anything like it! But you ought to have some others.

FLIP PALLOT — Yes, that's true, Lefty, because sometimes — particularly in tailing situations — the Clouser Deep Minnow isn't always the best choice. The other bonefish flies I like especially well are the Mother of Epoxy — you know, the epoxy fly with the vertical monofilament weedguards — and the Snapping Shrimp. I think if I could fish for bonefish with just three flies, it would be the Snapping Shrimp, probably on a #6 or #4 hook, the Mother of Epoxy on a #4 hook, and the Clouser Deep Minnow on a #6 or #4 with 5/32-inch and 6/32-inch eyes. Those would be the three. If you have those flies, I think you could go anywhere, worldwide, for bonefish.

LEFTY KREH — If you have the Clousers in the two colors I mentioned, the chartreuse and white and the tan and the white, I would agree with you absolutely.

FLIP PALLOT — And if I had to have two or three other flies for all my other saltwater work, they would be an offshore streamer, like a Lefty's Deceiver, which would work for all deep, saltwater situations . . .

LEFTY KREH — How about for redfish and snook?

FLIP PALLOT — This may sound nuts, but I use a Lefty's Deceiver for redfish, for snook, for tarpon — I use it for everything. But I use it in different configurations sometimes. Sometimes I use it on a bend-back hook. Sometimes I use it with a piano wire weedguard. But I always use a Lefty's Deceiver. I think the universal food in saltwater is minnows, and that's what the Deceiver imitates.

And you need a tarpon fly. Any of the standard tarpon flies are fine, I think. Again, as Dan said earlier, regarding tarpon — it's not so much what you feed them, it's how you feed them, because they need to eat all the time.

For permit, my fly of choice would probably be a Del's Merkin, in hook sizes from #2 up to 2/0, depending upon the size permit I was fishing for.

And that's really about it for saltwater flies, as far as I am concerned. But you've got to keep in mind, I am not one for millions of different flies. I keep it very, very simple. I am sure there are many other saltwater patterns that you can make a very good case for.

DAN BLANTON — I basically agree with Flip's choices. But remember, of course, there are lots of different kinds of saltwater fishing in different places.

One of the two best bonefish flies that I favor, in addition to those that Flip mentioned — I have fished it everywhere and know it works great — is called the Mini Puff. It's got a little chenille head with bead eyes and yellow and white grizzly hackle. I also take along the same fly in a tan or brown pattern, so that I can cover bonefish on both white sand and dark turtle grass bottoms.

As to my other bonefish choice, when I'm fishing at Christmas Island or Andros or Los Roques, all the Crazy Charlie patterns work well for me in hook sizes of #4, #6, and maybe even #8. The Crazy Charlie is what I refer to as an oceanic bonefish fly. It will work anywhere bonefish go.

On tarpon, if I only had one pattern to fish for tarpon, it would a standard tarpon fly in a brown and squirrel of some kind, like a Cockroach variation. I've caught tarpon on that pattern over white sand as well as over grass. It is rare that tarpon ever refuse it, at least in my experience. But I also think you need one bright tarpon fly, and the old standard — orange, yellow and grizzly — is about as good as you can get.

*If you had only a limited selection of flies with which to do all your fresh and saltwater fishing — seven, for example — which would they be, and why?*

DAN BLANTON — For trout fishing, even though I don't do as much as I like, I would first probably select some sort of general simulator nymph — you know, a *Callibaetis* nymph pattern. I would also choose a small Sparkling Caddis, because we have a lot of caddis on the Sacramento River where I do a lot of my trout fishing. But it's a great nymph to use anywhere, for that matter.

An Elk-hair Caddis would be my third selection. And I would definitely have a damselfly nymph pattern.

For my fifth fly, I would choose a general dry attractor. I have difficulty choosing between an Adams and a Humpy. Let's go with the Adams.

And I've got to have a Woolly Bugger, in black, olive, or purple. I mean, some people call it fishing with bait, but I don't care! It works!

Add a Muddler Minnow. I would always have a Muddler. I can fish a Muddler wet so that it resembles a bullhead or a small baitfish pattern. Or I can fish it dry like a hopper. I believe I can catch fish anywhere on a Muddler. That's my freshwater seven.

Now for my seven saltwater flies. The first on my list, without exception, is a Lefty's Deceiver, which is a pattern that resembles an elongated baitfish.

Next would be a pattern I designed, the Whistler, which is particularly suited for fishing saltwater areas where the water is turbid. But it also works well in clear water when you're trying to imitate the shorter-body baitfishes — the grunt, shad, and perch types.

The next is another of my designs, the Sar-Mul-Mac.

Then a good general baitfish simulator, a squid fly of

some kind. Squid are everywhere and saltwater game fish recognize and feed on squid all the time. The Sea Arrow Squid is one that I would use.

Next, some kind of popper. There are lots of styles, but I think something along the lines of a Skipping Bug would be my first choice.

As I've mentioned before, for my primary bonefish fly I would have a Mini Puff pattern, with the yellowhead white wing grizzly, or in a tan color.

For my tarpon fly, if I only had one tarpon fly to fish with, it would be a brown and squirrel Cockroach. And for permit, a Del's Merkin.

LEFTY KREH — Jim, are you going to list any flies?

JIM TEENY — Yes, I would like to. Actually more for me, because I am in a different situation. It wouldn't be just seven patterns for me, though, because I am more into the color. For my saltwater fishing, I would take our Teeny Leech pattern. It's a big fly, tied on 3/0 or 4/0 hook. But I would take it in seven different colors, so that it would look like seven different flies. To list them: black would probably first, then I would have the natural — which is a brown — hot pink — which Billy Pate calls fuchsia — orange, antique gold, ginger, and hot green.

LEFTY KREH — Hot green being the insect green?

JIM TEENY — No, it's not the insect green. Hot green is a bright green, a lime green. Although I have done well with the insect-green color, so maybe I should include that too.

DAN BLANTON — When you say bright, do you mean like a chartreuse green?

OVERLEAF: *An artificial and natural mayfly.*

JIM TEENY — Yes. And that's all I would do for saltwater, just change colors. Because I have enough confidence in the Teeny Leech pattern that I would just change the colors.

DAN BLANTON — When you're holding up your hand and describing the size of your Teeny Leech pattern, you're saying "this big." How many inches is that? Is that about two and a half inches? Our readers aren't going to be able to see your hands, Jim.

JIM TEENY — It's longer than that. It's pretty big, it's probably about three inches.

GARY BORGER — That's about four inches you've got laid out there now.

LEFTY KREH — But he's measuring fish right now!

GARY BORGER — Oh that's right! That's right!

JIM TEENY — Okay you guys! Then moving to freshwater, basically all I am fishing with are Teeny Nymphs — particularly the flash-fly pattern which only comes in three sizes, #2, #4, and #6, in two-tone with a little bit of Crystal Flash — more like an attractor pattern, along with the Teeny Leech.

When I am really seriously fishing, I seem to do better with just the nymph and leech patterns. When the fish are a little more difficult to get to bite, they will take the nymphs better. When they are more aggressive and are on a good take, they will take the leeches better. So, actually I'm offering them a different body structure and style, with different silhouettes and sizes. One is longer and narrower, and one is shorter and maybe a little fatter.

LEFTY KREH — Dave, are you ready with your list?

DAVE WHITLOCK — Yes. For freshwater — and I'm talking about trout here — my selections for floating patterns would be an Adams and a Royal Wulff.

For a partially-floating or underwater fly, a Muddler Minnow. The Muddler will get me by for a grasshopper or a stonefly imitation too, because I have fished it effectively on hatches like that.

For surface film as well as underwater presentations, a Black Ant. It's an awful good fly.

For my nymph pattern, I would go almost exclusively with a Red Fox Squirrel Nymph.

And I've got to have a Woolly Bugger, probably in black or dark olive.

And then, — and this may surprise you — a White Marabou Muddler, because I can fish it as a shad or a surface lure or a popper. The White Marabou Muddler, like the Muddler, is a very versatile fly. When you grease the head, you can fish it as a diver or as a streamer.

In saltwater situations, I would use a Whitlock's Diver Streamer, the Sheep Fly — which is a fly that I have lately been very impressed with — a Lefty's Deceiver, a Pencil Popper, a Seducer, a crab pattern, and a shrimp pattern.

LEFTY KREH — That sounds good! Johnny?

JOHN RANDOLPH — Well, there will be repeats, I am sure. For my dry flies, a Royal Wulff, a beetle pattern, an ant pattern, an Elk-hair Caddis, an Adams, and for stillwater presentations, a damselfly nymph pattern.

LEFTY KREH — You know what's interesting? When I put this question about seven flies before a group of professionals many years ago, I asked Dave to select first, and then I wrote down my seven, Dave had selected five of my seven. But I never seen a selection like this that did not include the Adams.

JOHN RANDOLPH — For underwater, I've got a lot of favorites, so I'm going to be over seven, counting the dry flys. Definitely the Woolly Bugger, a Hare's-Ear Nymph, a Pheasant Tail Nymph, the Muddler Minnow, and the Clouser Deep Minnow.

FLIP PALLOT — My freshwater choices would be: Royal Wulff, Elk-hair Caddis, an ant pattern, Muddler Minnow, a leech pattern, the Clouser Deep Minnow, and the Woolly Bugger.

My saltwater selections would be: Glass Minnow, Mother of Epoxy, Del's Merkin, Snapping Shrimp, Lefty's Deceiver, Clouser Deep Minnow, and Flip's Prince of Tides.

GARY BORGER — Well, the question says if you have only seven flies with which to do all your freshwater fishing? You can't do it with seven! I wouldn't even try it with seven!

LEFTY KREH — So you've listed more than that, right?

GARY BORGER — What you are really asking me is, are there just seven patterns that I can carry and feel comfortable in fishing in a lot of different places? But with that arbitrary minimum number, I wouldn't be able to do everything, mind you. Because if you are going to do everything, you cannot do it with seven flies, not in freshwater. For example, in my book on designing trout flies, I have 50 designs — 50! — tied in a lot of different sizes and colors, I consider that my minimum set for freshwater fishing.

LEFTY KREH — Hey Gary, we can't deal with a list that long!

GARY BORGER — Okay. So what I will give you is the list that I  think I would catch most of my trout on — let's say

80 percent of my fish. Here they are: a Strip Leech, a Hair Leg Nymph, a soft-hackle emerger pattern, a Yarn Wing Dun, a mayfly spinner pattern, a Hair Leg Wooly Worm, the Braided-Butt Damsel, the Marabou Damsel Nymph, the Borger Poly Caddis, the Griffith Gnat, the Brassie, the Sparkle Midge Pupa, along with one pattern each to represent an egg, an ant, a hopper, a scud and a snail; and finally, Lefty's ever present favorite, the dreaded San Juan Worm.

DAVE WHITLOCK — Boy, that's a big seven!

GARY BORGER — Can't do it in seven! I wouldn't even try!

LEFTY KREH — Well, I will try to do it in six!. The Griffith Gnat, Adams, Royal Wulff, Woolly Bugger, Clouser Minnow, and Elk-hair Caddis. And if I had to choose only three, they would be a Clouser Deep Minnow — it's the best all-around underwater fly I have ever fished — an Adams and a Woolly Bugger.

For the saltwater flies, my picks would be the Clouser Deep Minnow, the Whistler, the Deceiver, and like Dan, I like a Skipping Bug — I think you've got to have popping bugs! Add to that a Bend Back and a Crazy Charlie for all kinds of small things — everything from mangrove snapper to bonefish.

And just as Dan recommended, if I had to have one tarpon fly, it would be a Cockroach. But I also catch a lot of tarpon on Deceivers. And for permit, the Del's Merkin.

*Do you have favorite "super fly" patterns that you can always count on when the fishing gets tough?*

JIM TEENY — I do.

LEFTY KREH — Well, we ain't gonna ask you! You'd do anything to make money! Well, I think the world will now know that Jim Teeny uses nothing but Teeny Nymphs!

JIM TEENY — Since 1971!

DAN BLANTON — I have two selections for each type of water. I believe there are super freshwater flies, the Woolly Bugger and the Muddler Minnow and in saltwater, Lefty's Deceiver and my Whistler pattern.

GARY BORGER — There are some super flies that are useful, I think. Some are super flies in that they not only will catch several species but also they will represent a lot of different things. And if you want something that will represent a lot of things, let's put the Griffith Gnat at the top, because that baby is good for anything . . .

LEFTY KREH — You and I are in love with that fly!

GARY BORGER — Another super fly is a Strip Leech. I have caught everything that I have ever thrown it at. It's like the Clouser Deep Minnow, except that it's tied with a long strip of hair. It works underwater like crazy. Another of my super fly selections would be the patterns in the Hair Leg Nymph series. That series of flies will catch anything that eats insects. The Hair Leg Wooly Worm is another.

Another super fly is the Braided-Butt Damsel. It will work in any lake situation for any lake fish. It's a dry fly, but you can fish it wet, too. In fact, one of the secrets of using that fly is to fish it wet. It's just a killer when it's wet!

I would categorize hopper and scud patterns as being super flies, for both lake and stream situations, and for fishing to a wide variety of species.

FLIP PALLOT — My super fly selection would be Lefty's Deceiver, the Clouser Deep Minnow, Flip's Prince of Tides, and the Royal Wulff.

LEFTY KREH — My super flies are the San Juan Worm, the Clouser Deep Minnow, an egg pattern, and the Griffith Gnat. For a super dry, I would have to select the Adams.

In saltwater, if you had Clouser Deep Minnows, Skipping Bugs, Deceivers, and Whistlers in different colors and sizes, I think you could go most anywhere in the salt and catch all the fish you're going to catch.

DAVE WHITLOCK — I can take the Squirrel-hair Nymph in several sizes and configurations — from damselflies to scuds — and I can do well anywhere in the world.

But I have got an ace in the hole that I fish with almost exclusively when I really want to get really dirty with my fishing. It's a fly called the Near Nuff Sculpin. This little guy looks like a cross between a sculpin and a crayfish. It's tied primarily with a lead-eyed long-shanked hook. It rides with the hook up. It's dressed with a barred grizzly soft hackle or grizzly hackle tail. I also use the tan grizzly to palmer the body, with olive, black, and brown dubbing. It looks like a crayfish, and it looks like a sculpin. Because you know, there is an enormous amount of food that lives on the bottom of streams that trout or bass forage on. The Near Nuff Sculpin imitates those foods very well. You can fish it anywhere in the water column, or you can fish it on the bottom. I work it with a jigging action. It's deadly.

LEFTY KREH — Dave, I've got to tell you a story. You showed that fly to me, it must have been 10 or 15 years ago!

DAVE WHITLOCK — I've kept it a secret. It's so deadly!

LEFTY KREH — You told me not to say anything, so I never did. But I'll tell you a story about that fly. I had one with me one day when Trout Unlimited talked me into donating a day of my time to fish with two guys who had contributed money at a fund raiser.

We went to Big Hunting Creek in central Maryland. It's a little tiny stream just 10 or 15-feet wide. In a lot of places, you can almost jump across it. Anyway, these two guys had been fishing for about 30 minutes, without having any luck. Then we came to a big pool into which a big old tree had fallen. And they said to me, "Okay, Lefty, now let's see you fish." And I figured if there was going to be a decent fish anywhere in the neighborhood, it had to be under that tree. And keep in mind that before that day I had never seen a fish over 16 inches anywhere in that stream.

So I pulled out one of those Near Nuff Sculpins in a heavily weighted pattern. I cast it out and it went "Clonk!" up at the top of the pool. I started stripping until the fly reached an area just underneath the dead tree, and an 18 1/2-inch rainbow — which was the biggest rainbow I had ever seen in this water — came out from underneath the dead tree and grabbed that fly! These guys kept saying, "Awesome! Awesome!" And I have to confess, I had a big smirk on my face. As I was releasing the fish, they said, "Do it again!" And, of course, I had to try again, not really expecting anything. But then wham! . . . I get another hook-up from the exact same spot, a fish that measured about 16 inches! You might say that made my day!

DAN BLANTON — Well, a fly that I have caught a lot of freshwater striped bass on — one that has been particularly successful for me on the San Luis Reservoir — is your original Whitlock Sculpin, Dave. I would have to call it a super fly. This reservoir water holds a local forage fish called a blackfish, and your fly does a fantastic job of imitating it.

JOHN RANDOLPH — One reason I think this Sculpin pattern has been  so successful for you, Dave, is that almost none of our fly fishermen do much trout fishing on the bottom. It's virgin territory on a lot of our streams!

DAVE WHITLOCK — Let me add just one more observation. With the lead eyes that are on these flies, you can fish the bottom with a floating line.

LEFTY KREH — With this particular fly, instead of using sinking-line techniques, I agree with Dan. I would rather use a floating line with a long leader.

DAVE WHITLOCK — Well, we all know, Lefty, that a lot of fly fishermen just won't use a sinking line, so they have really limited themselves to the depth of water they can get down to and all the great fishing opportunities that are down there. But lead-eye patterns like this one will allow them to get down deep with a floating line.

LEFTY KREH — That thing really works. I had forgotten about it. I still have that in my box.

*Do fly fishermen carry too many flies?*

JIM TEENY — No!

DAN BLANTON — Not Jim anyway!

GARY BORGER — I think the initial reaction of the beginner is to carry too many flies. Because he doesn't understand what he should be doing with them. He will probably buy way too many — maybe because he just likes to own them — and jam them together in his fly box and not use them well. I think you're carrying too many fly patterns if you don't have a use for every single fly you have in your fly box.

LEFTY KREH — I think the more experienced you are, the fewer patterns you carry. But let me tell you about a law I've made for myself in that regard. I've learned this the hard way. If the fish have rabies and are biting some other guy's fly like crazy, but not mine, if the guy offers me one of his flies, I'm not going take it! He's going to have to give me two! A couple of times this has happened to me. I've been given a hot fly and have caught fish on it. But the fish tore the fly up so badly that by the end of the day I would end up with almost a bare hook. And with my weak memory, I had no way of duplicating the pattern when I got home! So I'm going to try to get two flies, if I can, and save one to take home to use for a model.

*Do you think that a fly body that sits flush on the surface is more or less appealing to trout than a fly that stands on its hackle tips, as conventional patterns do?*

LEFTY KREH — I find if I'm fishing very slow-moving water and there is no hatch on, I will catch a lot more fish on flies with a body that sits on the surface of the water — a thorax tie or haystack or paradun or something like that. I like this type of fly better than the conventional flies that stand up on their tippy-toes. Because I think that with a pattern of this type, in which the body of the fly is either on or very close to the surface, the fish get a better look at the fly. At least I know I have better luck with them.

GARY BORGER — Because that's the way the natural actually looks, Lefty.

But the answer to this question really depends upon what you're trying to imitate and the type of water you're fishing in. Let me give you an illustration. The Griffith Gnat, which is, without a doubt, the deadliest adult midge imitation ever developed, works! Not because it looks like a midge adult per se, but because it stands up on its hackle tips the way a midge adult stands up on its legs. The midge adult keeps its body well off the water. Its body never gets to the surface. And that's exactly what a Griffith Gnat does. When you look at the pattern from underwater — as it is sitting just outside the fish's window of vision — its hackle tips push down on the surface of the water exactly in the same way as do the legs of a natural midge. And that is the trout's trigger mechanism.

LEFTY KREH — If you are going to fish for trout with small flies, I think the Griffith Gnat is the single best fly there is! I tie the pattern both with and without the peacock herl body. Do you?

GARY BORGER — Yes.

LEFTY KREH — You gave me a tip one time. You told me that if you sometimes cut . . .

GARY BORGER — Oh, yes, what I do is cut the hackles off the bottom of the fly so that the weight of the hook pulls the fly down flush to the surface film to exactly imitate an emerging midge. This happens with most insects when they are emerging. I have photographed this lots of times. Let me show you what it looks like. *(See next page — Ed.)*

You can see that the husk of the insect is hanging right under the film, horizontal to the surface. When the insect first comes out, it has no definition. It looks just like a pencil sticking out of the husk. But then eventually, its wings unfold and it gets its legs out. Well, if you're fishing a Griffith Gnat with the bottom of the hackles trimmed off, as I have said, the hook causes the fly to sink down underneath the surface a little bit, with the hackle sticking up out of the top. It looks just like an insect crawling out.

LEFTY KREH — That's fabulous. I meant to thank you a couple of times for that!

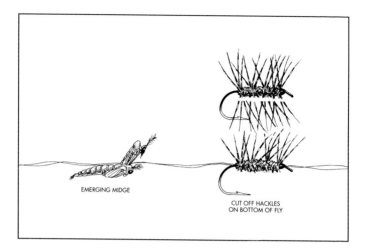

EMERGING MIDGE

CUT OFF HACKLES
ON BOTTOM OF FLY

*Gary Borger Modification to Griffith Gnat*

JOHN RANDOLPH — That's a good trick to try a lot of times on flat water, if the fish are not taking your fly, to clip off the hackle and . . .

LEFTY KREH — You mean regular flies.

JOHN RANDOLPH — Yeah, to get the fly into the surface film.

LEFTY KREH — I have found that flies that float flush in the film don't float as well and drown quicker. That won't work as well in fast water. I don't recommend that for fast water.

DAN BLANTON — So what you guys are basically saying to us is that both types of flies work well, depending upon the situation. The key is to make a presentation so that the fly operates as a natural would.

GARY BORGER — That's right! During heavy hatches fish will most often take the emergers. Simply because you can't run with your pants down!

LEFTY KREH — Run with your pants down! Get out of here, Borger! You can't run with your pants down!

GARY BORGER — That's why the Comparadun pattern works so well, why the no-hackles work so well, why the soft hackles fished dry on the surface work so well, why the floating nymphs work so well — because all of these flies are partly in the surface and partly out of the surface. They look like they are an emerging insect. And the fish just key in on that. It's amazing how they lock onto that.

*What are the basic criteria for good fly design?*

LEFTY KREH — How about you telling us about this Gary? Because even though you're sitting right here, I don't mind saying that your latest book on fly design* is absolutely one of the best jobs you have ever done!

GARY BORGER — But that's a whole book, Lefty! In fact, several books!

LEFTY KREH — I know it is. But we'll cut you off after a while, because it'll soon be time to go to lunch!

GARY BORGER — Okay, fair enough. Let me try to make it as simple as I can. I think good fly design means that when the fish sees the fly presented with the correct method, the fish thinks the fly is identical to whatever it's been eating — or is some other new food that looks to eat — and it eats it. And that's the way you can boil down what good fly design is. From there on, it's really all the technical information about how to design the parts of the pattern to make it look like a natural.

*Designing Trout Flies,* by Gary A. Borger (Tomorrow River Press, Publishers, P.O. Box 1745, Wausau, Wisconsin 54402, 1991).

We just went through that type of discussion with the Griffith Gnat, you'll recall. Since we know that an adult midge sits up high on the surface film, you want to construct an imitation that sits up high in the surface film. Emerging mayflies — as the drawing I made demonstrated — hang in the film with their body horizontal as their adult body emerges. So for that imitation, you want something that looks just like that. Or for some really great emerger patterns, you can tie a little chunk of foam sticking out in front. Or, since we know that an adult caddis sucks in an air bubble when it goes down, to imitate that behavior you can tie a fly with a little silvery-colored Antron wing on it to represent the diving caddis fly.

In line with this type of thinking, I recall that Gary LaFontaine has discovered that adult caddisflies on the surface have a certain kind of profile that is established by the width of their wings as they touch the surface of the water. So, to imitate that behavior, for that particular fly design you want to create a wing that yields that same kind of profile to the trout as it looks up.

Or on slow-moving waters, to give yet another example, when a trout sees an adult mayfly sitting on the surface, the wings sticking up over the back of the mayfly are very prominent and are a very easily seen feature. That's why you would want to create a winged pattern to represent mayflies on this type of water.

Or for example, to duplicate a spinner with cross-shaped wings, a cross-shaped profile is all important.

I can keep going on and on with examples such as this. But I think you get my point.

JOHN RANDOLPH — Let me ask you a couple of questions. What's more important, body color or wing color, or can you make that differentiation?

GARY BORGER — Yes, you can make that differentiation. You can talk about size, shape, color, and behavior as being the four major characteristics that fish key in when they are selectively feeding. All of these characteristics are important, but sometimes one is the primary trigger and sometimes the others are secondary triggers. It depends upon the situation at any given time.

Under bright-light conditions, a white wing is just as effective as a wing of any other color. Because under bright-light conditions, as the trout looks up from below at, say, a mayfly, the mayfly's wing looks white because of all the sparkling light that's being reflected off the surface of the water. The natural looks very, very white!

But under dull-light conditions, the natural will appear the same color that it actually is, so that under dull-light conditions, I like to use an imitation that's the same color as the natural. What I do is tie all these type patterns in various natural colors, because when you put the fly in bright light the wing's going to look white anyway. And for this I like to use real sparkly materials — like sparkle yarn and other kinds of things that reflect and refract light.

And this then leads to a consideration of the shape and the natural anatomy of the wing of the insect — what it's doing and how light is bouncing off its body. All of these things are characteristics that the fish watches closely, even though sometimes it doesn't see every single characteristic until the very last second before it commits itself to a take.

DAN BLANTON — Gary, what about flies that have all these characteristics you have just mentioned, and yet can be designed so that the angler can see them better? If I can't see this wonderful fly, it doesn't do me any good, because I don't know when I'm going to get a strike.

LEFTY KREH — I've got a tip on that. Last year, I started tying the wings of all my parachute flies with two strands of Crystal Flash. What I do with a parachute fly, for example, is that before I tie the wing on, I double it, double it, double it, and then I tie it on and make a post out of it. Then I go ahead and tie my fly and then when I am finished, clip off the excess Crystal Flash. That stuff is twisted at all angles, and as far out as 35 feet, I can see a #22 parachute fly with my 67-year-old eyes!

DAN BLANTON — You're using Crystal Flash to make the whole wing?

LEFTY KREH — The whole parachute wing! I got the idea from George Harvey. George is an older guy like me, and as you get older your eyesight gets worse. So you have to compensate. I usually use wings of fluorescent green or orange. I can see them better and I really don't think it makes any difference to the fish. Have you tried that, Gary?

GARY BORGER — Yeah, I use a lot of fluorescent colors in flies. Not so that I can see them better, but so the fish can see them better. And, you know, I've been doing work on color in flies for literally twenty years — twenty years of observing just how selective trout really are.

LEFTY KREH — Well, have you found that fluorescent wings produce fewer strikes?

GARY BORGER — No!

DAVE WHITLOCK — When I did that series on bright-spotted terrestrials, I found that the bright-spotted patterns actually outfished those same patterns in the same size and color — but without the bright spot on their backs — sometimes as much as three to one! Both types of patterns would be tied on the same leader, and yet the fish would take the bright one. I think it's because they can see it so much better.

LEFTY KREH — I never thought about the fish's viewpoint. But maybe that's why I'm getting more fish with these fluorescent applications.

JOHN RANDOLPH — The old golden rules that were inscribed in stone by the fly-fishing greats of yesteryear are sort of falling by the wayside these days.

GARY BORGER — But you see, John, they didn't have access to Crystal Flash and all these great fluorescent materials that we do. Just look at what the British are doing with their fluorescent flies! I mean, some of those patterns are absolutely weird, but do they catch fish!

I wish fluorescent materials in a wide range of colors — deep purple, white, and gray, for example — were more readily available here in the United States.

LEFTY KREH — Gary, you've done a lot of work on color. Why is it that purple and chartreuse, which I really don't see in a lot of fly patterns these days, are actually two of the best all-around colors to use in fly design?

GARY BORGER — Well, I believe it has to do with the way light is transmitted through water.

LEFTY KREH — I'm talking about underwater.

GARY BORGER — That's what I mean. Because as light passes through water, the red end of the spectrum is absorbed first. Within the first meter — or three feet — all of the red light has been absorbed. As depth increases, the other colors are quickly absorbed; blue light is transmitted the deepest. The deepest-growing algae in the ocean is 300 meters down, and it absorbs only blue light. That's why it looks red — it absorbs blue and reflects red. So, when the fly goes down deep, it's actually reflecting more light if it's purple. You see, "purple" means it's reflecting purple light, not absorbing it.

LEFTY KREH — Well, what about chartreuse, then?

GARY BORGER — Well, chartreuse is still carrying the green end of the spectrum, which is over closer to the blue than it is to the red, so it's easier to see.

LEFTY KREH — I mean, if I could only pick two Woolly Buggers, one of them would have to be purple.

GARY BORGER — Something else that's interesting. Look outside at the sky. I know it's gray out there today, but imagine there's a blue sky. Did you ever wonder why the sky is blue?

LEFTY KREH — No!

GARY BORGER — Because blue light . . . what's the matter with you, Lefty? . . . everybody wonders why the sky is blue! Because with blue light, the blue end of the spectrum is scattered more than any other. So when it comes into the atmosphere, blue light scatters. So you see blue light.

The same thing happens when light goes into the water. The red is quickly absorbed and the blue is scattered. So if you're underwater, looking through the water — if it's clear water — you're going to see blue — it's going to look blue. In producing videos, we've found that anytime you look through clear water, you have what's called background space light. Background space light is a silvery-blue color. Videos that have been shot underwater in clear water will always look silvery-blue in the background. A purple or chartreuse fly leaps out against that background. That's why fish appear to us as being of a silvery color. You look at most oceanic fish, they're silvery so that off in a distance . . .

LEFTY KREH — They're camouflaged . . .

GARY BORGER — . . . they're camouflaged against the background space light.

But now, if you look at water that has a lot of algae in it, you will find that the color of the background space light has changed, because now the algae is absorbing red and blue and giving out green. So now you have a greeny-blue background.

Look at bog water . . . that sort of tea-colored water . . . it has almost immediately absorbed the blue end of the spectrum. So from underwater it looks red, brownish-red.

So if you present the colors of purple and chartreuse against pale green, silvery, or brownish-red background colors, the purple and chartreuse colors will stand out well against all of them. That's also why flies with flash on them work so well in water, I think. You can see them against every background.

# THE SYMPOSIUM PARTICIPANTS' FAVORITE FLIES

## DAN BLANTON

"TOP SEVEN"

### Freshwater

Adams • A *Callibaetis* nymph pattern
A damselfly nymph pattern • Elk-hair Caddis
Muddler Minnow • Sparkling Caddis • Woolly Bugger

### Saltwater

Cockroach • Del's Merkin • Lefty's Deceiver
Mini Puff • Sar-Mul-Mac • Sea Arrow Squid
Skipping Bug • Whistler

"SUPER FLIES"

### Freshwater

Muddler Minnow • Whitlock Sculpin • Woolly Bugger

### Saltwater

Lefty's Deceiver • Whistler

## JOHN RANDOLPH

"TOP SEVEN"

### Freshwater

Adams • An ant pattern • A beetle pattern
Clouser Deep Minnow • A damselfly nymph pattern
Elk-hair Caddis • Hare's-Ear Nymph
Muddler Minnow • Pheasant Tail Nymph
Royal Wulff • Woolly Bugger

## LEFTY KREH

*Freshwater*

Adams • Clouser Deep Minnow • Elk-hair Caddis
Griffith Gnat • Royal Wulff • Woolly Bugger

*Saltwater*

Bend Back • Clouser Deep Minnow • Cockroach
Crazy Charlie • Del's Merkin • Lefty's Deceiver
Skipping Bug • Whistler

"SUPER FLIES"

*Freshwater*

Adams • Clouser Deep Minnow • An egg pattern
Griffith Gnat • San Juan Worm

*Saltwater*

Clouser Deep Minnow • Lefty's Deceiver
Skipping Bug • Whistler

## DAVE WHITLOCK

"TOP SEVEN"

*Freshwater*

Adams • Black Ant • Muddler Minnow
Red Fox Squirrel Nymph • Royal Wulff
White Marabou Muddler • Woolly Bugger

*Saltwater*

A crab pattern • Lefty's Deceiver • Pencil Popper
Seducer • Sheep Fly • A shrimp pattern
Whitlock's Diver Streamer

"SUPER FLIES"

*Freshwater*

Near Nuff Sculpin • Squirrel-hair Nymph

## GARY BORGER

*Freshwater*
An ant pattern
Borger Poly Caddis
Braided-Butt Damsel
Brassie
An egg pattern
Griffith Gnat
Hair Leg Nymph
Hair Leg Wooly Worm
A hopper pattern
Marabou Damsel Nymph
A mayfly spinner pattern
San Juan Worm
A scud pattern
A snail pattern
A soft-hackle emerger pattern
Sparkle Midge Pupa
Strip Leech
Yarn Wing Dun

"SUPER FLIES"

*Freshwater*
Braided-Butt Damsel
Griffith Gnat
Hair Leg Nymph
Hair Leg Wooly Worm
A hopper pattern
A scud pattern
Strip Leech

## FLIP PALLOT

*Freshwater*

An ant pattern • Clouser Deep Minnow
Elk-hair Caddis • A leech pattern
Muddler Minnow • Royal Wulff • Woolly Bugger

*Saltwater*

Clouser Deep Minnow • Del's Merkin
Flip's Prince of Tides • Glass Minnow • Lefty's Deceiver
Mother of Epoxy • Snapping Shrimp

"SUPER FLIES"

*Freshwater*

Clouser Deep Minnow • Royal Wulff

*Saltwater*

Clouser Deep Minnow • Flip's Prince of Tides
Lefty's Deceiver

## JIM TEENY

"TOP SEVEN" AND "SUPER FLIES"

*Freshwater*

Teeny Leech in different sizes
Teeny Nymph in flash-fly patterns

*Saltwater*

Teeny Leech in 7 Colors

Note: For further details regarding the favorite flies listed, including, for many patterns, recipes of materials needed and detailed tying instructions, see *Designing Trout Flies,* by Gary A. Borger (Tomorrow River Press, Publishers, P.O. Box 1745, Wausau, Wisconsin, 1991); *Dave Whitlock's Guide to Aquatic Trout Foods,* by Dave Whitlock (Lyons & Burford, Publishers, 31 West 21 Street, New York, New York, 1982); and *Salt Water Fly Patterns,* by Lefty Kreh (MARAL, INC., Producer, 2700 West Orangethorpe, Fullerton, California 92633, 1990).

# ILLUSTRATIONS OF ESSENTIAL FLY-FISHING KNOTS

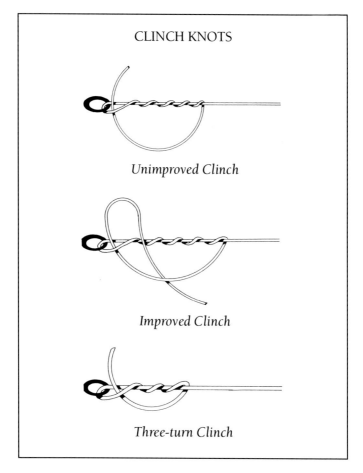

CLINCH KNOTS

*Unimproved Clinch*

*Improved Clinch*

*Three-turn Clinch*

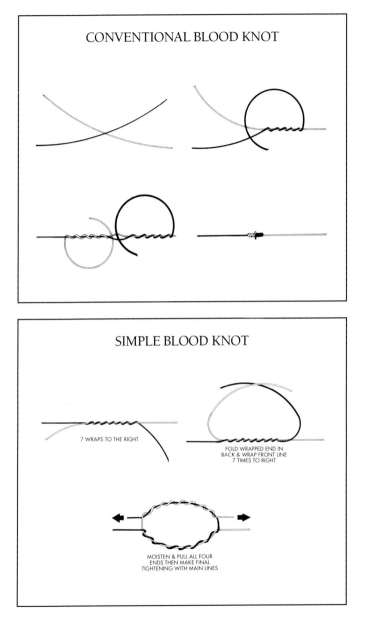

# CONVENTIONAL BLOOD KNOT

# SIMPLE BLOOD KNOT

7 WRAPS TO THE RIGHT

FOLD WRAPPED END IN
BACK & WRAP FRONT LINE
7 TIMES TO RIGHT

MOISTEN & PULL ALL FOUR
ENDS THEN MAKE FINAL
TIGHTENING WITH MAIN LINES

## STU APTE IMPROVED BLOOD KNOT

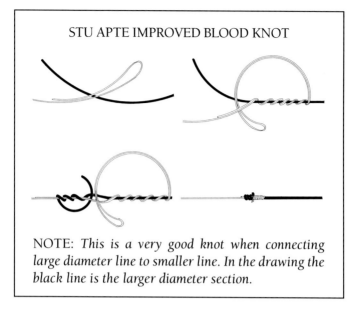

NOTE: *This is a very good knot when connecting large diameter line to smaller line. In the drawing the black line is the larger diameter section.*

## UNI-KNOT (DUNCAN LOOP)

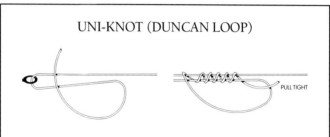

PULL TIGHT

## TRILENE KNOT

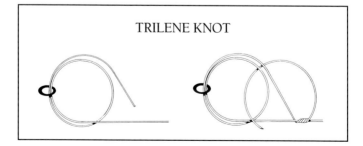

## NON-SLIP MONO LOOP

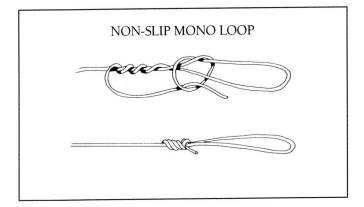

## PERFECTION LOOP

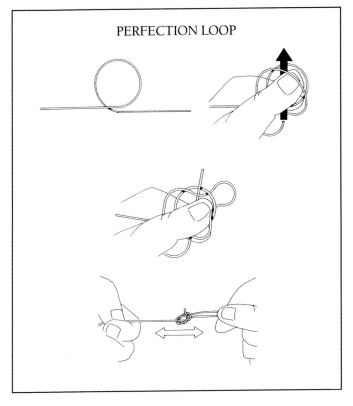

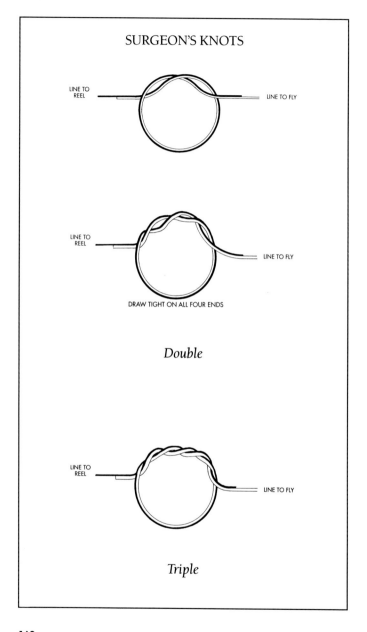

# SURGEON'S KNOTS

LINE TO REEL

LINE TO FLY

LINE TO REEL

LINE TO FLY

DRAW TIGHT ON ALL FOUR ENDS

*Double*

LINE TO REEL

LINE TO FLY

*Triple*

# SURGEON'S LOOPS

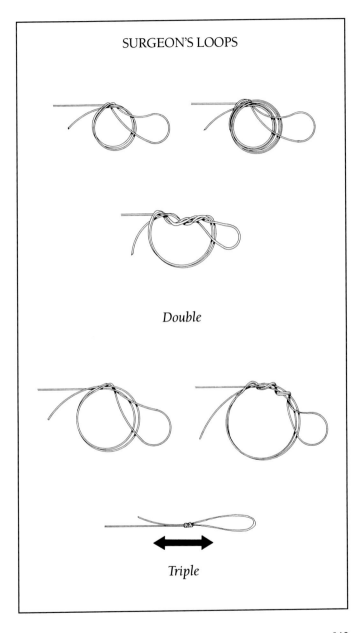

*Double*

*Triple*

# SPEEDY NAIL KNOT

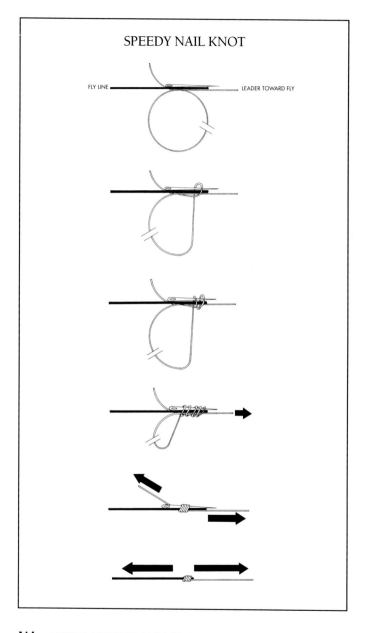

FLY LINE

LEADER TOWARD FLY

# GEORGE HARVEY DRY-FLY KNOT

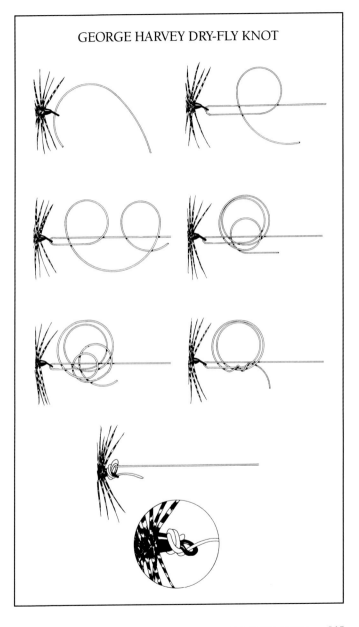

# BIMINI TWIST

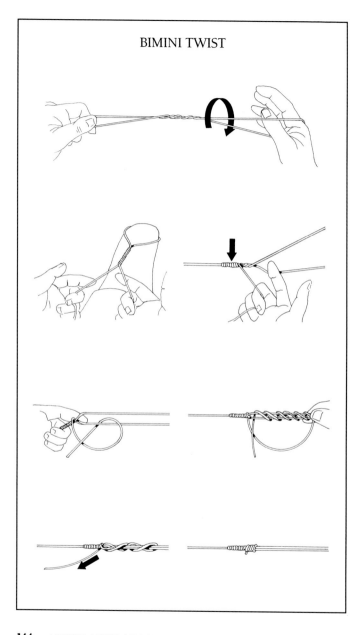

# HUFFNAGLE KNOT

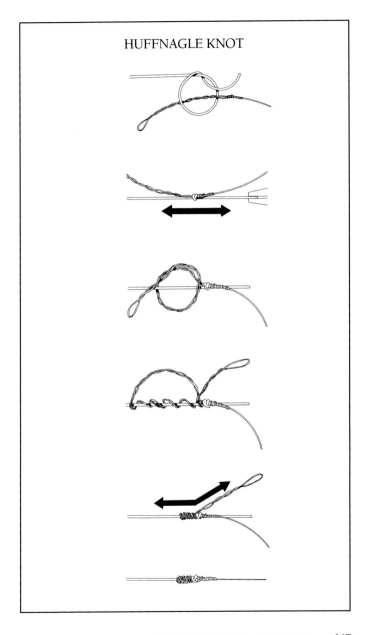

# HOMER RHODE LOOP KNOT
## (Step One)

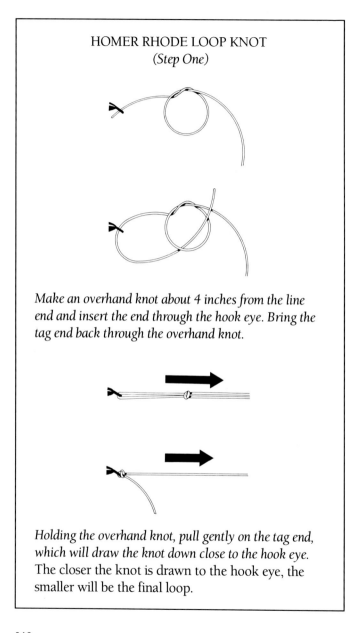

Make an overhand knot about 4 inches from the line end and insert the end through the hook eye. Bring the tag end back through the overhand knot.

Holding the overhand knot, pull gently on the tag end, which will draw the knot down close to the hook eye. The closer the knot is drawn to the hook eye, the smaller will be the final loop.

# HOMER RHODE LOOP KNOT
## (Step Two)

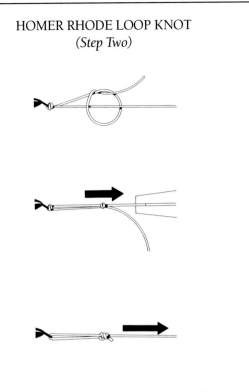

*Make another overhand knot around the main line. The closer this second overhand knot is to the hook eye, the smaller will be the loop. Firmly close the overhand knot with pliers and then pull on the main line. The overhand knot near the hook eye will slide up and bump against the second knot and form the loop.*

NOTE: *This is a weak knot, breaking at about 60 percent of line strength. It should only be used when connecting a shock tippet to the fly. It can also be used for tying braided wire leader material.*

# ALBRIGHT KNOT WITH A LOCK

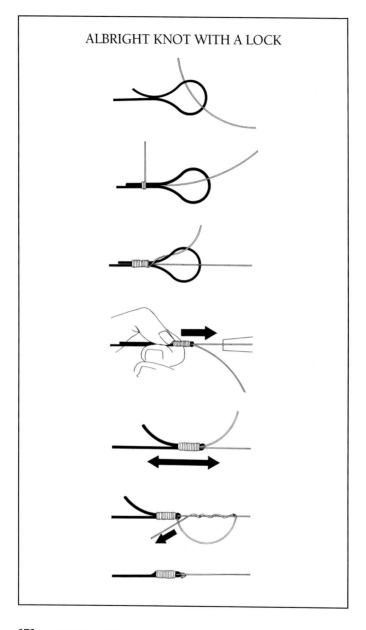

# INDEX